AFRO-AMERICAN EDUCATION, 1907–1932
A Bibliographic Index

AFRO-AMERICAN EDUCATION, 1907–1932
A Bibliographic Index

Richard Newman

Lambeth Press
New York

Lambeth Press
143 East 37th Street
New York, N.Y. 10016

First edition 1984

Library of Congress Cataloging in Publication Data
Newman, Richard.
　Afro-American education, 1907–1932.

　Includes index.
　1. Afro-Americans—Education—Indexes.　I. Title.
LC2801.N5　1984　　016.37'08996073　　83-24869
ISBN 0-931186-05-6

Printed on acid-free, 250-year-life paper
Manufactured in the United States of America

For Alicia Cummins;
and Lori, Jennifer, Brian,
and Bradford Newman

Contents

Preface   ix

Foreword, *Robert C. Morris*   xi

The Bibliography   1

List of Journals Indexed   115

Index   159

About the Author   179

Preface

For a quarter of a century, from 1907 until 1932, the U.S. Bureau of Education (which became the U.S. Office of Education in 1929) created annotated indexes to the vast literature acquired by its library. Consisting primarily of some 700 periodicals, this material also included pamphlets, monographs, conference papers, and government documents. It comprehensively covered everything written in the United States on education, as well as a great deal from foreign countries.

Over the years, some 45,000 citations to this literature, usually with full analytics, were published irregularly by the Bureau. They appeared in 117 bibliographies, under a variety of titles, some with annual author and/or subject indexes. As a result of the total lack of uniformity, however, they are extremely difficult to locate and use, even though they are unique: no other indexing of this information during this period exists. The Office stopped indexing in 1932 because the H. W. Wilson Company had begun publishing its *Education Index* in 1929.

The problem of access to this fugitive but important early material was solved only several years ago by Malcolm C. Hamilton of the Gutman Library at Harvard. He located and collected all 117 bibliographies, compiled a cumulated name and subject index, and supervised their facsimile reproduction. They were published in chronological order in twelve volumes under the title *Education Literature, 1907–1932* by Garland Publishing, Inc., of New York. At the time of its reprinting, *Library Journal* said the series was "The best single approach to an index service in education" since it contains "an incredible wealth of detailed information."

To create this present book, I carefully read all 45,000 entries in all twelve volumes of the reprinted bibliographies, and pulled the 461 citations which deal in one way or another with Afro-Americans, or Blacks in the Caribbean and Africa. These entries were then filed by author in one alphabetical sequence, with cross-references for secondary authors. Each entry was numbered. I then created an especially detailed and particular index.

The result is that access now exists in one volume to virtually all that was written on Afro-American education from 1907 to 1932. My hope is that it will serve as a useful tool for students, teachers, librarians, and researchers in the study of this vital but neglected period of Black history.

Richard Newman
New York, New York
September 1983

Foreword

The first three decades of the twentieth century represent a major transition in the history of Black education. It was a time not only of expanding public school facilities but of economic, political, and demographic changes affecting the very nature of education in the United States. A shift from philanthropy and self-help to public support, movement of large numbers of Negroes from rural to urban areas and from South to North, disfranchisement, the decline of industrial education, and the hardening of school segregation all contributed to a significant alteration of the nineteenth-century pattern. Already recognized as important, this transitional period has attracted even greater attention in the wake of the 1954 school decision and subsequent developments in the latter half of the twentieth century. Scholars have shown increasing interest in the issues of an era extending from the "Age of Booker T. Washington" to the Great Depression, issues such as accommodation, racial discrimination, the triumph of white supremacy, and the inherent inequality of the "separate but equal" doctrine overthrown by the Supreme Court in the *Brown v. Board of Education* decision.

Fortunately for those concerned with the educational history of this period, the United States Office of Education undertook the task of compiling and issuing indexes to select publications received by its library between 1907 and 1932. These indexes in turn form the basis for the present work by Richard Newman, a bibliographic index concerning Afro-Americans and education. From the nearly 45,000 citations in the Office of Education index, Newman has selected and indexed 461 entries on Black education both nationally and internationally. The compilation is obviously strongest for the United States but also includes valuable information on Africa, the Caribbean, and other relevant areas.

Detailed coverage for the United States begins with the Progressive period, when unparalleled improvement in public education was accompanied by a widening racial gap with regard to school facilities and opportunities. In Black education attention was at first focused on an accommodationist sectional relationship involving, most notably, Booker T. Washington, Northern philanthropists, and reformers from both sides of the Mason-Dixon Line. Several large foundations established between the early years of Reconstruction and the beginning of World War I worked to advance Negro education in the South. All appear in this index—the Peabody Education Fund, the John F. Slater Fund, the General Education Board, the Anna T. Jeanes Foundation, the Phelps-Stokes Fund, and the Julius Rosenwald Fund. These Northern-based philanthropies were generally acceptable to Southern whites for a number of reasons. They concentrated on such areas as industrial and vocational education, teacher training, and rural schools and homes. They made no attempt to impose racial equality or to challenge white supremacy. And they did little to promote equal distribution of public funds for education. Although Booker T. Washington was committed to the eventual integration of Negroes in American life, his public positions on educational, social, and political issues suited the conservative tenor of the Southern education movement. He established useful alliances with the Northern philanthropists and with upper-class Southerners in support of industrial education at such institutions as Tuskegee and Hampton. As indicated by the references in this index, Washington was a powerful force in Black education. His ascendancy, to quote W.E.B. Du Bois in 1903, was "easily the most striking thing in the history of the American Negro since 1876."

Education was at the heart of Booker T. Washington's gradualist self-help philosophy. Like his mentor Samuel Chapman Armstrong, he promoted vocational training as the most effective means of improving the economic and moral position of Negroes and thereby reducing prejudice and discrimination. In public pronouncements obviously designed to appeal to whites, this complex accommodationist leader maintained that practical education should take precedence over politics, civil rights agitation, or labor activism. Meanwhile, behind the scenes he secretly supported legal challenges to discrimination and became the era's most influential Black political leader in seeming contradiction to his own stated precepts.

Washington's critics saw a number of major flaws in his

educational doctrine. Du Bois objected to its economic emphasis and thought that it slighted higher education, while others pointed out that the manual skills taught in industrial programs were fast becoming outmoded in the face of new technological developments and increased discrimination against Black workers. The whole concept of industrial education came under close scrutiny.

Black higher education, on the other hand, was still in the early stages of development. In 1916 a United States Bureau of Education study prepared by Thomas Jesse Jones reported that only 33 of 653 Black institutions were teaching any subjects of "college grade." Of the 12,726 students attending these schools 1,643 were studying "college subjects" and 994 were in professional classes. The remaining 10,089 were in the elementary and secondary grades. Only three institutions of higher learning—Howard, Fisk, and Meharry Medical College—had "student body, teaching force, equipment, and income sufficient to warrant the characterization of 'college.'" Conditions began to change after World War I, however, as Negro enrollment in collegiate programs increased in both Black and white institutions and as universities such as Howard, Fisk, and Atlanta expanded their graduate programs.

Demographic changes in the early twentieth century affected education at all levels. In the South the large-scale movement of Blacks from rural to urban areas led to improved educational opportunities. Similarly, migration out of the region, especially after the beginning of World War I, had a considerable impact on the Northern states, where a growing number of Black students were absorbed into the schools. Although segregation and inequality existed in many Northern school systems as well as in those of the South, there were definite signs of progress in areas of development ranging from literacy to college attendance.

More extensive advances were precluded by prevailing racial views and policies. In the South especially the persistence of white supremacy guaranteed that segregated schools would be separate but not equal. By 1930 the racial gap in school support was as wide as it had ever been in a region with limited financial resources to devote to education. Between 1900 and 1930 the ratio of funds expended for white education compared to that spent on Blacks rose from 3:2 to 7:2. The differential subsequently decreased slightly, but as late as 1936 expenditures for Black students in the South represented just over one-sixth of the national average for all schools.

A careful reading of Newman's bibliographic index suggests the centrality of education in discussions of what was generally referred to as "the Negro question." For many, education was a safe and conservative answer to that crucial "question," related as it was to most racial matters under consideration, including the nascent area of mental testing, which came into its own in the early twentieth century with the development of academic tests by the College Entrance Examination Board and intelligence tests by the French psychologists Alfred Binet and Théodore Simon. The racial implications of mental measurement were underscored after World War I when information leaked out on the results of the Army's wartime testing program. Revealed in 1919, the disturbing statistics indicated that 47.3% of white draftees and 89% of Black draftees had a "mental age" of 12 years or under, raising serious doubts concerning the nature and extent of racial differences, the validity of the tests, and the role of education. Most of the pertinent articles listed in the index were published after these results were made known, and some of the titles are revealing: "The Intelligence of Negroes at Camp Lee, Virginia," "A Study of Ideals, Intelligence and Achievements of Negroes and Whites," "The Comparative Abilities of White and Negro Children," and "The Question of Negro Intelligence."

The scope of *Afro-American Education, 1907–1932* is broad enough to encompass this and most other major Black educational topics of the period. It will undoubtedly be an invaluable resource for those carrying out research in areas that definitely need further development.

Robert C. Morris
Schomburg Center for Research in Black Culture
The New York Public Library

The Bibliography

.

A

1. Abbott, Lyman. Can the Negro be educated? Outlook, 117: 602-604, December 12, 1917.

   An elaborate study of the report on Negro
   education, published by the U.S. Bureau of education.

2. Abbott, Lyman. Hampton revisited. Outlook, 119:
114-15, May 15, 1918.

   One of the series of Knoll papers. Describes
   the methods in vogue in Hampton school, Va.
   Discusses Negro education.

3. Abbott, Lyman. Letters to unknown friends: Negro
education. Outlook, 100: 115-16, January 20,
1912.

* Abbott, Lyman. See also 188.

4. Adams, Elbridge L. The Negro music school settlement. Southern workman, 44: 161-65, March 1915.

   Describes the work of the Music school settlement
   for colored people, New York city. Encourages
   among Negro pupils "the beauties and possibilities
   of their own racial music," etc.

3

* Adler, Felix. See 409.

5. Aery, William A. The school education at Hampton institute. Southern workman, 54: 130-36, March 1925.

6. Aery, William A. Teaching teachers at Hampton. Southern workman, 43: 430-36, August 1914.

   Describes manner of reaching, "through well-organized summer work, hundreds of earnest colored teachers who feel the need of Hampton's training."

7. African education commission. Education in Africa; a study of West, South, and equatorial Africa by the African education commission, under the auspices of the Phelps-Stokes fund and foreign mission societies of North America and Europe; report prepared by Thomas Jesse Jones, chairman of the commission. New York, Phelps-Stokes fund [1922]. xxviii, 323 p. incl. front., illus. (maps) plates. 8°.

   The African education commission spent nearly a year's time in 1920-21 in traveling through a great part of Africa and thoroughly studying the educational status of the natives. The results of the commission's investigations are given in this report.

8. Allen, A.T. North Carolina's school program. Southern workman, 52: 271-77, July 1928.

   Negro education in North Carolina described.

* Allen, A.T. See also 52.

9. Allen, E.H. The community's responsibility for
   health education in Negro schools. Bulletin
   (National association of teachers in colored
   schools), 12: 25-26, December 1931.

   States that each member of a community should
   aid in health education inasmuch as ill health
   affects each individual.

10. American academy of political and social science.
    The Negro's progress in fifty years. Philadel-
    phia, American academy of political and social
    science, 1913. 244 p. 8°. (Its Annals, vol.
    xlix, whole no. 138, September 1913.)

    Contents: Part IV, Educational progress and
    need--Negro illiteracy in the United States, by
    J.P. Lichtenberger; Negro children in the public
    schools of Philadelphia, by H.W. Odum; Higher
    education of Negroes in the United States by E.T.
    Ware; Industrial education and the public schools,
    by B.T. Washington; The Negro in literature and
    art, by W.E.B. Du Bois.

11. Andrews, Willie Dean. Negro folk games. Play-
    ground, 21: 132-34, June 1927. illus.

12. Applied knowledge as a problem in Negro education;
    by Hugh M. Browne. Washington, 1916. 6 p.
    (U.S. Bureau of education. Miscellaneous
    publication, September 1916.)

13. Arminjon, Pierre, and Crabites, Pierre. Al Azhar
    university. Nineteenth century, 98: 540-49,
    October 1925.

    Describes the famous old Mohammedan university
    at Cairo, Egypt.

14. Ashmore, Otis. A Savannah school of industry.
       Southern workman, 44: 485-90, September 1915.

       Work of the new Cuyler street school, Savannah,
     Ga., which has accommodations for one thousand
     pupils. Devoted to the industrial education of
     colored children.

15. Atwood, R.B. Kentucky faces the problem of
       training colored teachers. Kentucky Negro
       education association journal (official organ
       of the Kentucky Negro education association),
       1: 21-26, February 1931.

       A lack of funds is the chief cause of inadequate
     facilities for teacher training within the State.

16. Ayres, Leonard Porter. Seven great foundations.
       New York, 1911. 79 p. 8°.

       A collection of articles which were printed in
     the Journal of education during the fall of 1910.
       Contents: I. The Peabody education fund. II.
     The John F. Slater fund for the education of
     freedmen. III. The Carnegie institution of Wash-
     ington. IV. The General education board. V. The
     Carnegie foundation for the advancement of teach-
     ing. VI. The Russell Sage foundation. VII. The
     Anna T. Jeanes foundation.

B

17. Barbados. Reports, etc., of the Education de-
       partment, 1928. Barbados, T.E. King & company,
       1929. 106 p.

18. Barrett, Jane P. The Virginia Industrial school. Southern workman, 55: 353-61, August 1926.

 History and activities of the school are given. Illustrated.

19. Basutoland. The annual report of the Director of education for the year 1929. [1930] 28 p.

20. Berea college decision. Nation, 87: 480-81, November 19, 1908. Outlook, 90: 757-58, December 5, 1908.

21. Bermuda. Director of education. Report for the year 1930. Bermuda, Government printer, 1931. 30 p.

 The annual, official report on education in Bermuda.

22. Bibliography on education of the Negro. Comprising publications from January 1928 to December 1930. Compiled by Ambrose Caliver ... and others. Washington, United States Government printing office, 1931. 84 p. (U.S. Office of education. Bulletin, 1931, no. 17.)

23. Blascoer, Frances. Colored school children in New York. [New York] Public education association of the city of New York, 1915. 176 p. 8°.

* Blose, David T. See 370.

24. Bonham, M.J., Jr. Answer to the Negro question: education. Education, 28: 507-10, April 1908.

25. "Booker T. Washington." A symposium. Southern workman, 45: 35-56, January 1916.

    Contains appreciative sketches of B.T. Washington by W.T.B. Williams, D.H. Ramsey, W.P. Lawrence, Theodore Roosevelt, etc.

26. Botts, John M. Better schools on the way. Southern workman, 56: 474-78, October 1927.

    Discusses Negro education in the southern states.

27. Boyer, Philip Albert. The adjustment of a school to individual and community needs. Philadelphia, Pa., 1920. 141 p. tables. 8°.

    Thesis (Ph.D.)--University of Pennsylvania, 1920.
    A study of the Stanton-Arthur school, which serves a Negro section in Philadelphia.

28. Brady, St. Elmo. After-war program of Negro education. Tuskegee student, 30: 6-7, April 12, 1919.

*   Branley, Miguel A. See 262.

*   Bratton, T.D. See 63.

29. Brawley, Benjamin. The course in English in the secondary school. Southern workman, 45: 494-502, September 1916.

    A discussion of the English course for Negro schools.

30. Brawley, Benjamin. Early effort for industrial
    education. [n.p.] 1923. 15 p. 8°. (On
    cover: The trustees of the John F. Slater fund.
    Occasional papers, no. 22.)

31. Brawley, Benjamin G. Education. *In his* A short
    history of the American Negro. New York, The
    Macmillan Company, 1931. p. 132-46, 157-63,
    210-18.

    In the chapters devoted particularly to Negro
    education the author traces the work of various
    religious organizations and other groups in
    organizing schools for Negroes; discusses "The
    Tuskegee idea" of practical education; and pre-
    sents the following observations concerning self-
    help in Negro education: (1) the Negroes have
    paid in direct property and poll taxes approxi-
    mately $90,000,000 during the last 65 years;
    (2) they have contributed at least $35,000,000
    to education through their churches; (3) the
    Negro student probably pays a larger percentage
    of the running expense of the institution that
    he attends than any other student in the land.

32. Brawley, Benjamin. Ironsides: The Bordentown
    school. Southern workman, 60: 410-16, October
    1931.

    Gives a brief history and description of the
    work of the Manual training and industrial school
    for colored youth at Bordentown, N.J.

33. Brawley, Benjamin. A short history of the Ameri-
    can Negro. Rev. ed. New York, The Macmillan
    company, 1919. xvii, 280 p. 12°.

    The following chapters of this book deal with
    educational and cultural conditions of the Negro:
    IX. Missionary endeavor; XI. The Tuskegee idea;

XV. Self help in Negro education; XVI. Social
and economic progress; XVII. Literature and art.

34. British Guiana, Education department. Report of
the Director of education for the year 1929.
Georgetown, "The Argosy" company, ltd., 1930.
33 p.

35. Brock, George D. A study of the physical condition and comparative development of the colored
women teachers of West Virginia. Institute,
W. Va., The West Virginia collegiate institute,
1922. 11 p. fold table. 8°. (The West
Virginia collegiate institute bulletin, ser. 9,
no. 3. September 1922.)

* Brock, J.R.P. See 293.

* Browne, Hugh M. See 12.

36. Buck, J.L.B. Builders of a community. Southern
workman, 50: 172-77, April 1921.

The story of the prosperous Negro colony in
Suffolk, Va. Illustrated.

37. Bullard, R.L. Education in Cuba. Educational
review, 39: 378-84, April 1910.

38. Bullock, B.F. The present status of agricultural
education in Negro schools. Bulletin (organ
of the National association of teachers in
colored schools), 11: 4, 17-18, 24, April-May
1931.

Only the beginnings have been made in agricultural education in Negro schools, particularly in land-grant colleges, in which the major portion of this work is done. The author gives four precautions: (1) Warning against premature development; (2) need for placing emphasis where it is most needed; (3) possibility of the existence of a lack of sincerity; (4) the danger of making agricultural education too academic.

39. Bullock, Ralph W. A study of occupational choice of Negro high school boys. Crisis, 37: 301-303, September 1930.

The data were gathered from 1833 Negro high school boys in North Carolina, Tennessee, Georgia, Virginia, Missouri, and District of Columbia. The author finds a tendency for Negro high school boys to shift away from the occupations of their fathers (excepting the professions). Fifty-five per cent express a desire to follow some one of the professions as a life career, and only a small per cent show any interest in the technical and commercial fields. These choices have been made without a basis of information or exploratory experience, for practically none of the 200 schools studied had any form of vocational guidance. The author makes a plea for greater emphasis on vocational guidance on the part of high schools for Negroes.

40. Buttrick, Wallace. Baptist schools as promoters of Negro education. Missions, 11: 455-57, September 1920.

Address of the president of the General education board at the Buffalo convention of the Northern Baptist convention.
The progress in public school education for Negroes in the South and the forces and organizations that have brought this about.

41. Buttrick, Wallace. Enduring qualities of Booker
    Washington. Southern workman, 51: 550-54,
    December 1922.

    An address at the unveiling of the Washington
    monument at Tuskegee, Ala., April 1922.

C

42. Caliver, Ambrose. Bibliography on the education
    of Negroes. Washington, U.S. Government print-
    ing office, 1931. 34 p. (U.S. Office of edu-
    cation. Bulletin, 1931, no. 17.)

    Annotated references on different phases of
    education of Negroes for the years 1928-1930.

43. Caliver, Ambrose. Education of Negroes. *In*
    Biennial survey of education in the United
    States, 1928-1930. Chapter XVII. Education
    of certain racial groups in the United States
    and its territories. p. 37-56. Washington,
    Government printing office, 1931. (Bulletin,
    1931, no. 20, Chapter XVII.)

    This is an abbreviated survey of Negro education
    during the biennium 1928-1930. The five large
    divisions of the study are: Public education;
    higher education; accreditment; research and
    publications; and the creation of the new Federal
    service in the education of Negroes. The report
    shows great progress in the development of Negro
    education as well as wide discrepancies in the
    provision for equality of educational opportunity.
    In the States maintaining separate school systems
    the schools for Negro children are kept only

three-fourths as many days as are the schools
for white children. In 1928 there were 282 coun-
ties without high school facilities in which the
Negro population was 12½ per cent or more of the
total population. Transportation facilities are
relatively negligible. While school enrollment
and attendance has increased greatly during recent years, the distribution of students in the
various classes is disproportionate. 74 per cent
were enrolled in the first five grades in 1928
and only 3.7 per cent in the high school. Tables
and graphs present statistics on enrollment, income and expenditure, distribution of schools,
term length, popularization of secondary education, salaries and accredited schools.

44. Caliver, Ambrose. The integration of secondary
        and higher education. Bulletin (official organ
        of the National association of teachers in
        colored schools), 12: 7-8, 26; 7-9, 28-29,
        October-December 1931.

        Describes and illustrates graphically the his-
        torical growth of the college and the high school
        and indicates past and present trends in the
        relationships between them.

45. Caliver, Ambrose. The largest Negro high school.
        School life, 17: 73-74, December 1931.

        Describes the physical plant and discusses a few
        innovations in the internal administration and
        community activities fostered by the Birmingham
        Industrial high school of Birmingham, Ala.

46. Caliver, Ambrose. Negro schools and American
        education week. Washington, U.S. Office of
        education, 1931. 10 p. Mimeographed. (Circu-
        lar no. 43.)

Reports activities of Negro schools in American education week for previous year; presents general program for current year, with bibliography for reference and figures to show progress made in education in recent years.

47. Caliver, Ambrose. Progress of the National surveys of education among Negroes. School and society, 35: 231-34, February 13, 1932.

Reports the progress of the three national surveys being conducted by the U.S. Office of education, viz., The National survey of secondary education, The National survey of the education of teachers, and the National survey of school finance, as they relate to the education of Negroes. The facts revealed by these studies should contribute much toward the advancement of education.

* Caliver, Ambrose. See also 22.

48. Cape of Good Hope. Department of public education. Report of the Superintendent-general of education for the year ended 31st December, 1930. Cape Town, Cape Times, limited, 1931. 78 p.

This official report is written in plain, direct language easy for persons not acquainted with the Cape school system to understand. It deals with such topics as centralization of schools, extension of free education, organization of the system, and medical inspection. It is not overburdened with statistics. Any school teacher, particularly a rural-school teacher, will find it worth reading.

49. Carney, Mabel. African letters. Printed privately for students and friends who did so much to make my trip possible and the source of rich enjoyment it proved. [1926] 28 p. illus. 4°.

50. Carr, William G. Public education in the South. School and society, 33: 488-95, April 11, 1931.

   The theme of this article is found in its first sentence: "The boys and girls of the Southern States are to-day receiving an educational opportunity which is seriously inferior to that provided in the Nation as a whole." No specific treatment is given the Negro situation; but tables give data for both white and Negro conditions, and in addition, there is a comment or two by the author serving to fix the fact that the southern Negro children are not only a part of an inferior educational situation, but that they are also further handicapped by being subjected to conditions inferior to the inferior.

51. Carter, Thyra. Racial elements in American history textbooks. Historical outlook, 22: 147-51, April 1931.

   Analysis of eight textbooks to determine content and space given to the various nationality groups. Rank of nationalities in order from most to least space accorded was found to be: English, Germans, Irish and Scotch-Irish, Italians, and Poles.

52. Catawba college, Salisbury, N.C. The college. Three addresses. Salisbury, N.C., Catawba college, 1926. 23 p. 8°. (Catawba college bulletin, new ser., vol. 1, no. 4, January 1926.)

Contains: 1. What a college can do for its students, by A.T. Allen.--2. The function of a college, by J. Henry Highsmith.--3. The administration of the college curriculum in the light of modern educational philosophy, by Elmer R. Hoke.

53. Catholic educational association. Report of the proceedings and addresses of the sixteenth annual meeting, St. Louis, Mo., June 23-26, 1919. Columbus, Ohio, Catholic educational association, 1919. 590 p. 8°. (Catholic educational association bulletin, vol. 16, no. 2, November 1919.) (Rev. F.W. Howard, secretary, 1651 East Main St., Columbus, Ohio.)

Contains: 27. T.W. Turner: Actual conditions of Catholic education among the colored layman, p. 431-40.

54. Chapman, P.W. Problems and progress in Negro education. Southern workman, 60: 325-29, July 1931.

The chief problem in Negro education in Georgia is the retention of pupils through grades in which fundamental processes are taught. Progress has been made in the program of agricultural education conducted by the State. The author expresses the belief that if Negro children can be kept in school until they have obtained the fundamentals of a general education and, added to that, training in some vocation in which there is opportunity for employment, steps will have been made in solving the economic problems of the individual and in aiding the prosperity of the State.

55. Charléty, S. L'enseignement professionel des indigènes en Tunisie. Revue pédagogique, 64: 421-48, May 1914.

55A. Christian education in Africa and the East, with
     an introduction by Sir Michael Sadler. London,
     Student Christian movement, 1924. viii, 116 p.
     16°.

     Contents: The Western contribution to education
     in Asia and Africa, by J.H. Oldham. Christian
     education in Africa, by J.H. Oldham.

56. Clark, J.L. Race relations course in a state
     college. Southern workman, 59: 55-57, February
     1930.

*   Claxton, P.P. See 188.

57. Colding, Ursula S. A unique public school.
     Southern workman, 59: 401-408, September 1930.

     The purpose of the author is to give a descrip-
     tion of the activities in the Paul L. Dunbar
     school of Norfolk, Va., where provision is made
     for over-age pupils in grades one to six in the
     Negro schools of the city.

58. Coleman, Satis N. The drum book. New York,
     N.Y., John Day Company, inc., 1931. VIII,
     190 p. illus.

     This book deals exclusively with drums and tells
     how the drum is used in other lands. In Africa
     a code system has been developed and signals are
     sent to distant places by use of the drum. The
     different kinds of drums used by various nations
     are described. Suggestions as to how to make and
     use drums are made, and how to read drum music.
     The book is of particular value to teachers and
     parents who wish to promote creative music among
     children.

59. Coles, C.E. The land, the people, and the schools
of South Africa. Quarterly journal of the University of North Dakota, 7: 184-94, 351-65,
January, July 1917.

   The author was formerly missionary-superintendent
of schools in South Africa.

60. Collmann, Robin D. The psychogalvanic reactions
of exceptional and normal children. New York,
N.Y., Teachers' college, Columbia university,
1931. 88 p. (Contributions to education, no.
469.)

   Compares psychogalvanic reaction of 100 gifted,
110 normal, and 100 feebleminded children, all
white, and also 100 children of Negro blood.
Sex, age, race, etc., all carefully controlled.
Normal group significantly above both gifted and
feebleminded; Negro group significantly higher
than normal white; gifted only slightly above
feebleminded.

61. Colony of the Bahamas. Board of Education. Annual
report, 1919. Nassau, Nassau Guardian, Ltd.,
1930. 14 p.

62. Colony of the Gambia. Annual report of the
Superintendent of education for the year 1929.
Bathurst, Government printer, 1930. 26 p.

63. Conference for education in the South. Proceedings of the eleventh conference. Memphis,
Tenn., April 22-24, 1908. [Memphis, 1908]
231 p. 8°. (Edgar Gardner Murphy, secretary,
Montgomery, Ala.)

   Contains: 7. T.D. Bratton--The Christian South
and Negro education, p. 83-91.

64.   Conference for education in the South. Proceed-
        ings of the twelfth conference, Atlanta, Ga.,
        April 14-16, 1909. Nashville, Tenn., The Ex-
        ecutive committee of the Conference [1909].
        235 p. 8°. (Wickliffe Rose, secretary, Nash-
        ville, Tenn.)

        Contains: 14. C.L. Coon: Public taxation and
        the Negro school, p. 157-67.

65.   Conference for education in the South. Proceed-
        ings of the fifteenth meeting, Nashville, Tenn.,
        April 3d, 4th, and 5th, 1912. Washington, D.C.,
        The Executive committee of the Conference [1912].
        339 p. 8°. (P.P. Claxton, secretary, Washing-
        ton, D.C.)

        Contains: 11. W.D. Weatherford: Negro training
        in the South, p. 101-73.

66.   Cooke, Dennis H. The Negro rural-school problem.
        Southern workman, 60: 156-60, April 1931.
        tables.

        This article reports a study of 25 counties in
        North Carolina to ascertain the facts on school
        availability for Negroes. It was found that:
        (1) The problem of poor school attendance is
        greater in counties whose population is dominantly
        Negro; (2) as the per cent of Negroes in the total
        population decreases, the problem of the average
        per capita cost of instruction increases; (3) the
        per cent of 1-room Negro schools and the percentage
        of Negroes in the total population vary inversely;
        (4) it is a greater financial burden per pupil
        enrolled for counties having less than 10 per
        cent Negro population to provide buildings commen-
        surate with larger per cent of Negro population in
        other counties; (5) library facilities are slightly
        better in counties having 10 per cent Negro popula-
        tion than in other counties with greater Negro
        population.

67. Cooke, Dennis Hargrove. The white superintendent
       and the Negro schools in North Carolina. Nash-
       ville, Tenn., George Peabody college for teach-
       ers, 1930. 176 p. 8°. (Contributions to
       education, no. 73.)

     The general purpose of the author is: 1. To
     give a brief history of the development of public
     schools for Negroes in North Carolina; 2. to draw
     a picture of the status of public education for
     Negroes in North Carolina in 1928-1929; 3. to pre-
     sent the activities of the superintendents with
     regard to organizing, administering, and super-
     vising Negro schools; 4. to correlate activities
     of superintendents and the factors representing
     status of Negro schools in 1928-1929; 5. to ascer-
     tain the superintendent's philosophy of Negro
     education; and 6. to determine whether his
     theory and practice of Negro education coincide.

68. Cooley, Rossa Belle. The grown folks come to
       school. Survey, 60: 470-74, 485, August 1,
       1928.

     Describes adult education among the Negroes of
     St. Helena Island, N.C. [*sic*].

69. Cooley, Rossa Belle. A mission of love and
       literacy. Survey, 59: 443-51, January 1, 1928.

     Describes the history and activities of the
     Penn school of South Carolina, the first school
     for Negroes in the South.

70. Cooley, Rossa Belle. School acres, an adventure
       in rural education. New Haven, Conn., Yale
       university press, 1930. 158 p.

     Penn school, about which this volume is written,
     is not a trade school, nor merely an agricultural

school; it tries to equip boys and girls for life in the country and to dovetail the life of the South Carolina sea island into the teaching. The account is descriptive and shows how homes and farms were connected with the school, and how a rural life was enriched by a type of industrial education similar to that of Hampton and Tuskegee institutes.

71. Cools, G. Victor. Negro education and low living standards. Educational review, 72: 102-107, September 1926.

Criticizes the over-emphasis of professional education among Negroes. Urges industrial training in order to build up a competent middle class among the Negro race.

72. Cools, G. Victor. The problem of the Negro schools. School and society, 20: 168-73, August 9, 1924.

73. Cools, G. Victor. Why Negro education has failed. Educational review, 68: 254-59, December 1924.

Contends that Negro education must shift its emphasis from the classical and professional to the creative industry.

74. Coon, Charles L. Public taxation and Negro schools. Cheyney, Pa., Committee of twelve for the advancement of the interests of the Negro race [1909]. 11 p. 8°.

Paper read before the Twelfth annual conference for education in the South, Atlanta, Ga., April 14-16, 1909.
"A somewhat careful study of this question for

several years leads [the author] to the conclusion
that the negro school of the South is no serious
burden on the white taxpayer."

*   Coon, Charles L.   See also 64.

75.   Cooper, Clayton S.   The schools of Egypt.   World's
       work (London), 22: 647-51, November 1913.

       Discusses educational conditions in modern
       Egypt.   Shows widespread illiteracy.

*   Cooper, F.I.   See 280.

*   Cooper, Hermann.   See 76.

76.   Cooper, Richard Watson, and Cooper, Hermann.
       Negro school attendance in Delaware; a report
       to the State board of education of Delaware.
       Bureau of education, Service citizens of Dela-
       ware.   Newark, Del., University of Delaware
       press, 1923.   xxxii, 389 p.   front., illus.,
       tables, diagrs.   4°.

       The findings on the subject as presented in
       this report are statistical facts of interest to
       educational administrators wherever located.
       This study is to be followed by a similar one
       for the white schools of Delaware.

77.   Cooper, William John.   The Negro and education.
       Bulletin (National association of teachers in
       colored schools), 12: 15-16, 30, December 1931.

       The article states that the Negro to survive
       and advance must have an education that will
       prevent his forming so large a part of the largest

class of unemployed--the domestic servants; that
will enable him to farm intelligently and profit-
ably; that will give him more to sell than brawn,
which commodity is more and more becoming dis-
pensable. Emphasis must be placed upon capacities
and potentialities rather than handicaps.

78. Corson, David B. Tuskegee institute.... School
exchange, 5: 354-59, April 1911. illus.

79. Corson, O.T. Booker T. Washington, an appreciation. Ohio educational monthly, 65: 151-55,
April 1916.

Address before the Department of superintendence, National education association, Detroit,
February 25, 1916.

* Corson, O.T. See also 279.

* Crabites, Pierre. See 13.

80. Not used.

* Crabtree, J.W. See 278.

81. Cromwell, Otelia; Turner, Lorenzo Dow; and Dykes,
Eva B. Readings from Negro authors for schools
and colleges. New York, Harcourt, Brace and
company, 1931. 388 p.

A textbook of literary writings by Negroes embracing selections of poetry, short stories,
one-act plays, essays, and public addresses,
with suggestions for study and an extensive bibliography of additional works by Negroes.

D

82. Dabney, Charles. William Penn school, St. Helena
    Island. Southern workman, 60: 277-81, June
    1931. illus.

    A description of the events of April 15, 1931,
    at Penn school, the date upon which a bas-relief
    memorial of Doctor Frissell of Hampton was un-
    veiled, and the new building given by the General
    education board was dedicated.

83. Dabney, Thomas L. Negro schools in a Virginia
    county. Southern workman, 57: 37-41, January
    1928.

    Discusses the activities of the Virginia indus-
    trial school for colored girls, and the Virginia
    manual labor school for colored boys, of Hanover
    county, Va.

84. Dabney, Thomas L. Negro students in London uni-
    versities. Southern workman, 56: 517-20,
    November 1927.

85. Dale, Maud. Education in Egypt. Independent
    education, 2: 13-18, January 1929.

86. Daniel, Robert P. Basic considerations for valid
    interpretations of experimental studies pertain-
    ing to racial differences. Journal of educa-
    tional psychology, 23: 15-27, January 1932.

    From his discussion the author concludes "that
    (1) most studies so far reported are worthless as

indicating anything regarding the comparative mental ability of races; (2) most of our present techniques give measures of differences due to weaknesses in educational opportunities rather than of differences in mental ability; (3) there is need of a re-evaluation of the problems and methods of studies pertaining to racial differences."

87. Davis, J.E. Hampton at Penn school. Southern workman, 46: 81-89, February 1917.

Work of Hampton graduates at Penn school, St. Helena Island, off the coast of South Carolina.

88. Davis, J.E. Tuskegee institute and its conferences. Southern workman, 43: 157-67, March 1914.

An illustrated article on Tuskegee, describing its varied activities, with a résumé of the annual conferences held there this year. Address of Dr. B.T. Washington, and discussions.

89. Davis, J.E. A unique people's school. Southern workman, 43: 217-30, April 1914.

Describes the Penn school, St. Helena Island, South Carolina.

90. Davis, J.E. A Virginia asset: the Virginia industrial school for colored girls. Southern workman, 49: 357-64, August 1920.

91. Davis, Jackson. Building a rural civilization. Some educational results among southern

Negroes. Southern workman, 49: 501-508, 549-62,
November, December 1920. illus.

I. County training schools in the South.--
II. Supervising industrial teachers.

92. Davis, Jackson. Building a rural civilization.
Some educational results among Southern Negroes.
[Hampton, Va., Hampton institute, 1920.] 17 p.
illus. 8°.

Reprinted from the Southern workman for November and December 1920.
Contains: I. County training schools. II. Supervising industrial teachers.

93. Davis, Jackson. County training schools. Southern
workman, 47: 481-89, October 1918.

Describes the county training schools for
Negroes, in the Southern States--under the
auspices of the Slater fund and the General
education board. Illustrated.

94. Davis, Jackson. Negro training and racial good-
will. American review of reviews, 58: 521-28,
November 1918.

A résumé of the various activities of Hampton
institute, Va. Illustrated.

95. Davis, Jackson. New head of the Jeanes and Slater funds. Southern workman, 60: 404-406,
October 1931.

Presents a biographical picture of Dr. Arthur
D. Wright, the new head of the Jeanes and Slater
funds.

96. Davis, Jackson. The outlook for Negro colleges.
    Southern workman, 57: 129-36, March 1928.
    tables.

    Address given at the annual meeting of the
    Negro organization society in Norfolk, Va.,
    November 9, 1927.

97. Davis, Jackson. The Phenix school. Southern
    workman, 60: 264-68, June 1931. illus.

    An address delivered at the cornerstone laying
    of the Phenix demonstration school, erected by
    Hampton institute and the General education board
    as a practice school for teacher-training, and
    dedicated to George P. Phenix.

98. Davis, Jackson. Practical training in Negro
    rural schools. Southern workman, 42: 657-71,
    December 1913.

    A paper read before the meeting of the Southern
    educational association, Nashville, Tenn.,
    October 30 to November 1, 1913.

*   Davis, Jackson. See also 368.

99. Davis, John W. Platform for teachers in colored
    schools. Bulletin (National association of
    teachers in colored schools), 12: 5, 24, Decem-
    ber 1931.

    The author presents in 14 points "background
    thought" as a basis for consideration of a fac-
    tual and critical study of education as it affects
    Negroes.

100. De Bunsen, Victoria. The international conference on African children: a survey and a
forecast. Revue Internationale de l'enfant,
11: 3-11, Janvier 1931.

The author sketches briefly the story of Eglantyne Jebb, foundress of the Save-the-children
fund; the statement adopted by the League of
nations in 1924 with regard to the rights of the
child, now known as the "Declaration of Geneva";
and the plans for holding an international conference on African children in 1931.

101. A declaration of principles by representative
Negroes of North Carolina, Raleigh, September
26, 1919. Raleigh, N.C., Office of superintendent of public instruction, 1919. 12 p. 8°.

The declaration given in this pamphlet was
adopted by a conference of leading Negroes
called by Dr. E.C. Brooks, State superintendent
of public instruction, with a view to inaugurating
a broad educational policy for both races in
North Carolina and promoting confidence and
harmony.

102. Dillard, James H. Fourteen years of the Jeanes
fund, 1909-1923. [Durham, N.C., 1923.]
p. 193-201. 8°.

Reprint from the South Atlantic quarterly,
vol. 22, no. 3, July 1923.

103. Dillard, James H. The Jeanes fund. Independent,
67: 1250-52, December 2, 1909.

104. Dillard, James H. National aid to Negro education. School and society, 7: 669-71, June 8,
1918.

Abstract of a paper submitted at the Atlantic
City meeting of the Department of superintendence,
March 1, 1918.

105. Dillard, James H. The Negro goes to college.
World's work, 55: 337-40, January 1928.

106. Dillard, James H. Negro rural schools. Southern
educational review, 6: 303-308, February, March
1909.

* Dillard, James H. See also 278, 366, 377.

107. Dillon, A. Barrow. Compulsory education in
British Honduras. Oversea education, 1: 53-55,
January 1930.

108. Dixon, J.C. Negro high-school development in
Georgia. High school quarterly, 20: 30-32,
October 1931.

Since 1924, the date of the accreditment of
the first Negro high school meeting requirements,
14 public and 15 private high schools for
Negroes have been accredited. The General education board, the Anna T. Jeanes foundation,
the John F. Slater fund, the Rosenwald fund,
and the Commission on interracial cooperation
have contributed much to the development of
Negro education in Georgia. School buildings
are well equipped; teachers' homes, vocational
buildings, transportation, libraries, and aid
from various sources are available to those
interested enough to inquire about them.

109. Doggett, Allen B., jr. Hampton's school of agriculture. Southern workman, 53: 189-98,
November 1924.

110. Dougall, W.C. Training visiting teachers for African village schools. Southern workman, 57: 403-14, October 1928.

   Describes the activities of the Jeanes school at Kabete Kenya Colony, Africa.

111. Douglass, H. Paul. Problems and programs of Negro education. *In his* Christian reconstruction in the South. Boston, The Pilgrim press [1909]. p. 265-302.

112. Dowd, Jerome. The Negro in American life. New York, London, The Century co. [1926]. xix, 611 p. 8°.

   Contains: Chap. 21, Public-school education, p. 149-61. Chap. 22-23, Institutions of higher learning, p. 162-75. Chap. 64, Education as the solution, p. 498-501.

113. Du Bois, Rachel Davis. Building tolerant attitudes in high-school students. Crisis, 40: 334, 336, October 1931.

   Description of a project designed to build tolerant attitudes in high-school students, using seasonal events to develop the program embraced in the year's slogan, "The contribution of various races to our complex American life."

114. Du Bois, W.E.B. Education. Crisis, 40: 350, October 1931.

   Editorial comment on educational situations among Negroes in the Canal Zone, New Orleans, La., and in Muskogee, Okla.

115. Du Bois, W.E.B. Negroes in college. Nation, 122: 228-30, March 3, 1926.

*   Du Bois, W.E.B. See also 10.

116. Dunbar-Nelson, Alice. Negro literature for Negro pupils. Southern workman, 51: 59-63, February 1922.

117. Dyson, Walter. The founding of Howard university. Washington, D.C., Howard university press, 1921. 24 p. fold. plan. 8°. (Howard university. Studies in history, no. 1, June 1921.)

E

*   Eagleson, B.M. See 217.

118. Edwards, Thomas J. Helping Negro boys in Virginia. Southern workman, 46: 490-99, September 1917. illus.

    Excerpts from address delivered before the Virginia conference of charities and correction, Staunton, Va., 1917, on the work of the Negro reformatory at Broadneck farm, Hanover county, Va.

119. Elder, Alfonso. Analysis of some major problems connected with freshmen. North Carolina teachers record, 2: 25+, March 1931.

A study was made of 154 freshmen, 83 women and
71 men, boarders and day students. Ranks at-
tained in intelligence tests showed change of
position upon administering objective tests at
the end of quarter. It was assumed that students
whose standard achievement scores were not up to
their standard intelligence quotient scores had
not worked to the limit of their capacity.

120. Eleazer, Robert B. Negro education in Georgia.
      Spelman messenger, 43: 14-15, April 1927.

      Presents statistics of Negro education.

121. Ellis, G.W. Education in Liberia. (U.S.--
      Education, Comm'r of. Report for 1905.
      1: 111-29.)

      The author is United States secretary of lega-
      tion at Monrovia.

122. Embree, Edwin R. How Negro schools have ad-
      vanced under the Rosenwald fund. Nation's
      schools, 1: 37-44, May 1928. illus. plans.
      map.

      Shows how the great foundation is bettering
      the colored race by helping to provide adequate
      schoolhouse facilities in the South.

123. Embree, Edwin R. Julius Rosenwald fund--review
      for the year. Chicago, Julius Rosenwald fund,
      1930. 31 p.

      This study deals with: 1. the Negro front--the
      progress made by the Negro since the Civil War;
      2. the part played by the Rosenwald fund in the
      education of Negroes from the establishment of
      the first Rosenwald school in 1913, to the com-

pletion of the five thousandth school June 10,
1930. It summarizes the Fund's contributions to
trade schools, State colleges, private colleges,
fellowships, Negro health, child study, libraries,
general education, and grants made to other
agencies. Mention is made of the work done by
the State agents for Negro schools and the Jeanes
supervisors, the General education board, and
the Slater and Phelps funds.

124. Embree, Edwin R. Learning the new civilization.
In his Brown America, the story of a new race.
New York, The Viking press, 1931. p. 60-137.

The author presents a historical sketch of
Negro education under the captions, Sporadic
education during slavery, A Kentucky crusader,
Mission schools, Public schools, and Strategic
college centers. There is appended a bibliography of books by and about the Negro that "may
prove most interesting and profitable to the
lay reader."

125. Evans, Henry R. Educational boards and founda-
tions--1928-1930. Biennial survey, chapter
XXI. Washington, U.S. Government printing
office, 1931. 9 p. (U.S. Office of education.
Bulletin, 1931, No. 20.)

This is a section of the Biennial survey of
education in the United States, 1928-1930.
Contains (a) General education board; (b) Rockefeller foundation; (c) Carnegie corporation of
New York; (d) Carnegie foundation for the advancement of teaching; (e) Jeanes fund; (f) John F.
Slater fund; (g) Phelps-Stokes fund; (h) Commonwealth fund; (i) Julius Rosenwald fund; etc.

F

126. Farm training for Negroes. The essential factor in colored education in the South. Survey, 38: 267-68, June 23, 1917.

    A review of Dr. Thomas Jesse Jones' report on Negro education, published as a bulletin of the U.S. Bureau of education.

127. Farr, T.J. The intelligence and achievement of Negro children. Education, 51: 491-95, April 1931.

    Gave Illinois intelligence scale, Monroe standardized silent-reading test, and Monroe general-survey test in arithmetic to 200 Negro children. A small per cent of Negro children remain in school until they finish the eighth grade.

128. Favrot, Leo M. Aims and needs in Negro public education in Louisiana. [Baton Rouge, La., 1918]. 26 p. 8°. (Department of education, State of Louisiana. Bulletin no. 2, September 1918.)

    By the state agent of rural schools for Negroes under direction of T.H. Harris, State superintendent.

129. Favrot, Leo M. Negro education in Coahoma county, Mississippi. Southern workman, 54: 489-96, November 1925.

130. Favrot, Leo M. Negro school attendance.
Southern workman, 53: 9-13, January 1924.

Emphasizes the poor attendance in Negro
schools of the South.

131. Favrot, Leo M. Provisions for preparation and
training of Negro teachers. Bulletin (official
organ of the National association of teachers
in colored schools), 11: 15-16, January 1931.

A brief presentation of provisions for preparation and training of Negro teachers in 17
southern states. The agencies, needs, and
comparisons of facilities for teacher training
are discussed.

132. Favrot, Leo M. Some facts about Negro schools
and their distribution and development in
fourteen southern states. High-school quarterly, 17: 139-54, April 1929.

133. Favrot, Leo M. Some problems in the education
of the Negro in the South and how we are
trying to meet them in Louisiana. Baton
Rouge, Ramires-Jones printing co., 1919.
16 p. 8°.

Address before the National association for
the advancement of colored people, Cleveland,
Ohio, June 25, 1919.

134. Favrot, Leo Mortimer. A study of county training schools for Negroes in the South. Charlottesville, Va., 1923. 85 p. diagrs.,
tables (partly fold.). 8°. (The trustees
of the John F. Slater fund. Occasional
papers, no. 23.)

135. Favrot, Leo M. Training teachers for rural
     schools for Negroes. Arkansas school journal,
     18: 13-15, March 1913.

     Claims that in addition to the general require-
     ments in scholarship, professional training,
     and personal attributes, a teacher of a rural
     school should possess a love of nature, an
     understanding of rural activities, and a knowl-
     edge of the art of rural industries.

*   Favrot, Leo M. See also 283.

136. Ferguson, George O., jr. The intelligence of
     Negroes at Camp Lee, Virginia. School and
     society, 9: 721-26, June 14, 1919.

     Gives the results of the mental tests given
     to the soldiers at Camp Lee. Says the "intelli-
     gence quotient" of the Negroes was 77 per cent
     of that of the whites.

137. Ferguson, George O., jr. The mental status of
     the American Negro. Scientific monthly, 12:
     533-43, May 1921.

     Says that as yet comparatively little of a
     scientific nature has been done in investigating
     the mind of the Negro. Concludes that the men-
     tal differences between whites and Negroes, in
     general, shows that there should be a difference
     in the organization of the schools of the two
     races. "Psychological study of the negro in-
     dicates that he will never be the mental equal
     of the white race."

*   Fisher, Isaac. See 280.

*   Flexner, Abraham. See 188.

138. Frazier, E. Franklin. A community school....
      Southern workman, 54: 459-64, October 1925.

      Describes the Fort Valley and Industrial
      school [*sic*], Peach county, Ga.

139. Frazier, E. Franklin. Danish people's high
      schools and America. Southern workman, 51:
      425-30, September 1922.

      Describes the extended people's high school at
      Askov, Denmark, and discusses the possible value
      of similar schools in the southern states.

*   Frissell, H.B. See 281.

G

140. Gandy, John M. Educational reconstruction.
      Southern workman, 50: 38-42, January 1921.

      Discusses educational reconstruction and wel-
      fare work among Negroes, with emphasis on the
      profession of teaching.

141. Gandy, John M. Public high schools for Virginia
      Negroes. Southern workman, 53: 305-11, July
      1924.

142. Gardner, Katherine. Changing racial attitudes. Crisis, 40: 336, October 1931.

Discussion of the work of a Philadelphia high-school teacher in changing racial attitudes through a course in "Problems of democracy."

143. Garth, T.R. Race psychology. New York, McGraw-Hill book company, 1931. xiv, 260 p.

An excellent summary and discussion of studies in race psychology. The main conclusions, according to the author, are: (1) Selection operates in man as well as elsewhere; (2) the races of men are mobile; (3) nurture changes native traits.

144. Garth, Thomas R.; Lovelady, Bert E.; and Smith, Hale W. The intelligence and achievement of southern Negro children. School and society, 32: 431-35, September 1930.

The study investigates the extent to which educational achievement influences group intelligence scores of southern Negro children. Summarizes as follows: 1. Mental-growth line of Negro children starts at same point as whites but lags behind with increasing years. Retarding factor is not public stress; 2. Educational retardation is 61.1 per cent. Retardation less in upper than in lower grades; 3. MA of Negroes lower than that of whites; 4. CA of Negroes above that of whites; 5. "The educational age is above that of the mental age of the Negroes, and the achievement ratio is consistently above that of whites, on the average of 103"; 6. Correlation between intelligence and factors of education combined is quite high, .81. Little left for other factors; 7. School grade and educational achievement have equal weight in influencing intelligence scores.

145. General education board. Annual report ...
     1928-1929. New York, General education board
     [1930]. 113 p. 12°.

     Contains: Negro education, p. 23-37.

146. General education board. Annual report, 1929-
     1930. New York, General education board,
     1931. xv, 75 p. tables.

     Contains: Reports of the activities of the
     year of: III. Negro education: respecting Negro
     education, the activities in colleges and uni-
     versities, medical education and nurse training,
     junior colleges, normal and industrial schools,
     state-controlled institutions, state agents for
     Negro rural schools, fellowships, the John F.
     Slater fund, and the Anna T. Jeanes foundation.

147. Gillard, J.T. Negro education. Commonweal,
     11: 419-20, February 12, 1930.

148. Gold Coast colony. Annual report of the Educa-
     tion department for the year 1928-1929.
     Accra, Government printing office, 1929.
     27 p. chart.

149. Gore, George W., jr. A brief survey of public
     education in Tennessee. Broadcaster (official
     journal of the Tennessee State association of
     teachers in colored schools), 3: 52-53,
     January 1931.

     Status of public education for Negroes in
     Tennessee.

150. The government studies Negro education. Southern
     workman, 60: 500-502, December 1931.

Editorial dealing with radio speech of Doctor Caliver concerning the National surveys being conducted by the government.

151. Graham, Virginia Taylor. Health studies of Negro children. I. Intelligence studies of Negro children in Atlanta, Ga. Washington, Government printing office, 1927. 25 p. tables. 8°.

Reprint no. 1127 from the Public health reports December 3, 1926, pages 2759-2783.

152. Granges, Lester B. "Ironsides": the Bordentown (N.J.) vocational school. Southern workman, 56: 223-31, May 1927.

153. Grant, Cora DeForest. Ruggedness, the fourth "R" in Negro education. Nation's schools, 1: 55-59, February 1928. illus.

154. Greene, Harry W. Freshman week in Negro colleges. Christian educator, 26: 1-2, November 1927.

*   Gregg, J.E. See 171.

155. Grenada. Annual report on the Education department for the year 1928. Granada, Government printing office, 1929. 17 p.

156. Grose, Howard B. A glad day at Spelman seminary. Missions, 10: 338-59, May 1920. illus.

Pages 344-59 are devoted entirely to pictures showing the work that is being done in educating the Negroes at Spelman seminary, Atlanta, Ga.

157. Grymoult, Pierre. L'Université de Fez et les intellectuels marocains. Mercure de France, 140: 691-707, June 15, 1920.

158. Guest, L. Haden. Pioneer education in Rhodesia. New era, 12: 51-54, February 1931.

   An illustrated, descriptive article about the small schools in Rhodesia.

*   Guy, J.R. See 368.

H

159. Haile, A.J. Christian industrial training in South Africa. Missionary review of the world, 52: 443-48, June 1929.

160. Hall, H.N. The art of the Pullman porter. American mercury, 23: 329-35, July 1931.

   Gives experiences of Pullman porters with side lights on their selection, training, and compensation.

161. Hammond, Lily H. In the vanguard of a race. New York, Council of women for home missions and Missionary education movement of the United States and Canada [1922]. 176 p. front., plates, ports. 12°.

162. The Hampton institute trade school. I. Carpentry and cabinetmaking. Southern workman, 42: 271-79, May 1913. illus.

163. The Hampton institute trade school. Southern workman, 45: 153-60, March 1916.

   Seventh article of a series treating of the educational activities of the school at Hampton, Va. Treats of painting. Other articles have appeared as follows: Carpentry and cabinet-making, May 1913; blacksmithing and wheelwrighting, January 1914; bricklaying and plastering, April 1914; machine work, January 1915; tailoring, April 1915; and plumbing and steamfitting, December 1915. Illustrated.

164. Hampton Negro conference. Eleventh annual report. 109 p. Hampton, Va., The institute press. Published as the Hampton bulletin, vol. 3, no. 3.

   W.T.B. Williams; Colored public schools. p. 39-53.

165. Hampton Negro conference. Twelfth annual report, 1908. Hampton, Va., Hampton institute press, 1908. 73 p. 8° (The Hampton bulletin, v. 4, no. 3. September 1908. quarterly.)

   Contains: 1. P.C. Parks--Does an agricultural education pay? p. 24-27. 2. W.T.B. Williams--Negro schools and educational progress in the South, p. 52-66. 3. T.C. Walker--How to arouse the interest of the community in schools, p. 67-70. 4. M.N. Work--How to fit the school to the needs of the community, p. 70-73.

166. Hampton Negro conference. Report of the 13th annual meeting, 1909.

Contains: Community work done by schools for negroes, by W.T.B. Williams.

167. Hampton, Virginia. Normal and agricultural institute. Every-day life at the Hampton normal and agricultural institute. Hampton, Va., The press of the Hampton normal and agricultural institute, 1909. 32 p. illus. 8°.

168. Hampton normal and agricultural institute, Va. Fiftieth annual report of the principal. Southern workman, 47: 273-312, June 1918.

Historical and pedagogical review of Hampton institute, Va. Illustrated.

169. Hampton normal and agricultural institute. Its evolution and contribution to education as a federal land-grant college; prepared under the direction of Walton C. John. Washington, U.S. Bureau of education, Government printing office, 1923. 118 p. illus. 8°. (Bulletin, 1923, no. 27.)

170. The Hampton S.A.T.C. Southern workman, 48: 64-72, February 1919.

An illustrated article on the students' army training corps of the Hampton normal and agricultural institute, Va.

171. Hampton's semi-centennial. Southern workman (semi-centennial number), 48: 257-324, June 1919.

Account of the proceedings of the semi-centennial of Hampton normal and agricultural institute, Va., May 1-2, 1919. Speeches by J.H. Kirkland, M. Ashby Jones, R.R. Moton, W.H. Taft, etc. Contains fifty-first annual report of the institute by J.E. Gregg.

172. Hancock, Harris. The education of the colored race is the duty of the nation. Popular science monthly, 72: 452-64, May 1908.

*   Hanus, Paul H. See 188.

173. Hart, Albert Bushnell. White education; Negro education; Objections to education. *In his* Southern South. New York and London, D. Appleton and company, 1910. p. 288-337.

174. Hart, Joseph K. A new school every week: Delaware sets the pace in educational progress. Survey, 50: 573-75, September 1923.

Describes the new Booker T. Washington school at Dover, Del., which serves also as a community center for the Negroes all over the State.

175. Hartshorn, W.N., ed. An era of progress and promise, 1863-1910. The religious, moral and educational development of the American Negro since his emancipation. Boston, Mass., The Priscilla publishing co., 1910. 8, viii, 576 p. illus. 4°.

176. Harvey, B.C.H. Problem of the colored student. Journal of the Association of American medical colleges, 4: 208-22, July 1929.

177. Hayford, Adelaide C. A girls' school in West
Africa. Southern workman, 55: 449-56, October
1926.

Describes work in a Negro school in Sierra
Leone, British west African colonies.

178. Haynes, George E. Negroes move North. I. Their
departure from the South. Survey, 40: 115-22,
May 4, 1918.

First paper of series. Presents reasons for
Negro exodus to North and other parts of the
country. Cites lack of educational advantages
in the South as one of the reasons for migrating.

179. Hemphill, J.C. Problems of Negro education.
North American review, 206: 436-45, September
1917.

Discusses the report of Dr. Thomas Jesse Jones
of the Bureau of education on Negro education.

180. Henderson, Bertha, and others. An outline of
the courses in geography in the University
elementary school. Elementary school journal,
18: 186-205, November 1917.

Third paper of series; to be continued. Takes
up studies of South America and Africa, for sixth
grade children, who are asked not only "to ex-
plain the life conditions of a region by a study
of the controlling physical conditions, but to
make, from a study of these physical conditions,
their own inferences regarding life-conditions."

181. Hevia, Aurelio. General Leonard Wood and public
instruction in Cuba. Inter-America, 4: 3-16,
October 1920.

Describes the constructive work in education
accomplished during General Wood's administration of Cuba, 1899-1902. Work of Dr. E.J. Varona.

182. Hewitt, A. Comparative study of white and
colored pupils in a southern school system.
Elementary school journal, 31: 111-19, October
1930.

Ninety colored and 85 white seventh-grade
pupils were studied. Effort was made to equi-
librate groups in terms of grouping, supervision,
etc. The author draws the following conclusions:
1. Greater emphasis should be placed on language
work, both in elementary schools and teacher-
training schools for Negroes; 2. Curricula in
schools for Negro children should provide
greater opportunity for them to examine actual
material and to enlarge their perceptual experiences; 3. Wider use should be made of the
6-3-3 plan for Negro children; 4. It appears
"that teachers and supervisors of colored
schools, and probably instructors of colored
normal schools are inclined to accept a type
of work which is not tolerated by instructors
in white schools." "The evidence seems to point
to an unequal advantage for the slow group of
colored children. Equal opportunity demands
that the more intelligent Negro child be given
opportunity for advancement. More careful
grading, more objective comparisons, and higher
standards than are found would probably serve as
inducements for the intelligent colored children
to put forth effort commensurate with their
ability."

* Highsmith, J. Henry. See 52.

183. Hill, Leslie O. The Negro teacher in the after-
      math of the war. Howard university record,
      13: 112-17, March 1919.

      The substance of an address delivered at
      Witherspoon Hall, Philadelphia, Pa., January 31,
      1919, in the interest of the Cheyney training
      school for teachers.

184. Hill, W.B. Rural survey of Clarke county,
      Georgia, with special reference to the Negroes.
      [Athens, Ga., 1915]. 63 p. illus. 8°.
      (Bulletin of the University of Georgia, vol.
      15, no. 3. Phelps-Stokes fellowship studies,
      no. 2.)

185. Hill, William Bancroft. The American university
      at Cairo [Egypt]. Missionary review of the
      world, 47: 269-76, April 1924. illus.

      This institution is doing in Egypt what Robert
      college is doing in Constantinople, and what
      American university (formerly the Syrian Protes-
      tant college) is doing in Beirut.

186. Hoernle, A.W. An outline of the native concep-
      tion of education in Africa. Africa, 4: 145-
      63, April 1931.

      An attempt to outline certain fundamental
      aspects of the African cultures as a basis for
      aiding their educational development.

18/. Hogan, W.E. Changing conceptions of the aims of
      Negro education. Bulletin of the Board of edu-
      cation of the Methodist Episcopal church,
      South, 7: 116-24, November 1917.

      Presents certain changes that have occurred
      in the aims, methods, and content of Negro

education from the beginning of colored schools
in America to the present time.

*   Hoke, Elmer R.   See 52.

188. Hollis Burke Frissell.   Southern workman, 46:
      561-648, November 1917.

      Entire number is devoted to a symposium on the
      life and labors of Dr. Frissell, principal of
      Hampton Institute, Va., from 1893 to 1917. Dr.
      Frissell died August 5, 1917. Among the contrib-
      utors to the memorial number are: F.G. Peabody,
      P.P. Claxton, W.H. Taft, Paul H. Hanus, Lyman
      Abbott, Abraham Flexner, etc.

189. Holloway, William H.   Mechanic or dynamic?
      National note-book, 1: 21-24, April 1919.

      The attitude of the country toward cultural
      and higher education for the Negro.

190. Holmes, D.O.W.   The present status of college
      education among Negroes. Bulletin (official
      organ of the National association of teachers
      in colored schools), 11: 5, January 1931.

      Writer gives a brief review of efforts at
      standardization of Negro colleges from survey
      conducted by Jones in 1916 to present. Status,
      in terms of enrollment, size and training of
      faculties, salaries, income, libraries, and
      consolidations, is presented.

190A. Holt, Elizabeth G.   Negro industrial training in
      the public schools of Augusta, Ga. Journal of
      home economics, 4: 315-23, October 1912.

*   Honter, R.F.   See 197.

*   Hoover, Herbert.   See 321.

191.   Hope, John.   Negro school and community.   Atlanta,
       Ga., Atlanta university, 1932, 8 p.

       "Extending far beyond desk and blackboard, the
       influence of the Negro teacher reaches out into
       the homes of the pupils, and often makes all the
       difference between a good and a bad community."

192.   Hope, John.   Trained men for Negro business.
       Opportunity, 9: 343-45, 350, November 1931.

       How Atlanta university is meeting the need
       for trained Negro business men.

193.   Not used.

194.   Hrdlička, Aleš.   Children who run on all fours
       and other animal-like behavior in the human
       child.   New York, McGraw-Hill Book Company,
       1931.   418 p.

       The book includes reports of 369 individuals
       of the white race and 18 of other races who
       exhibited this type of behavior.   The emphasis
       of course is mainly anthropological but the
       book also gives insight into the development of
       locomotion.

195.   Huffington, J. Walter.   Supervision of colored
       schools in Maryland.   Baltimore, Issued by
       State department of education [1919].   35 p.
       8°.

* Hughes, E.L. See 366.

* Hunter, W.S. See 316.

I

196. Iles, R.E. Standardizing the Negro college. Peabody journal of education, 6: 96-101, September 1928.

197. Imperial education conference. Report, 1911. London, Published by H.M. Stationery office, Printed by Eyre and Spottiswoode, ltd., 1911. 267 p. 8°.

Contains: 10. R.F. Honter: Notes on the psychology of the Negro child and on the adaptation of primitive customs, manners, laws, and traditions in a system of education, p. 228-37.

J

198. Jackson, W.C. College instruction in race relations. Religious education, 26: 123-26, February 1931.

The removal of prejudice is a problem of education--an educational task of vast proportions. A list of schools offering courses in interracial relationships is given.

199. Jacobs, Emma S. Pioneering in home economics among the Negroes of Tidewater, Virginia. Journal of home economics, 21: 85-91, February 1929.

200. Jamaica. [Education department]. Annual report of the Education department for the year 1929-30. Kingston, Government printing office, 1931. 60 p.

    The official annual report of education in Jamaica.

201. Jamaica. Education department. Annual report of the education department for the year ended 31st December, 1930. Kingston, Government printing office, 1931. 58 p.

    An unusually good official report in which the school system is described in some detail and the statistical data for the year are given.

*   John, Walton C. See 169.

202. John F. Slater fund. Proceedings and reports for the year ending September 30, 1915. 64 p. 8°.

203. The John F. Slater fund. Proceedings and reports of the John F. Slater fund for the year ending September 30, 1926. 25 p. 8°. (Miss Gertrude C. Mann, secretary, Box 418, Charlottesville, Va.)

204. John F. Slater fund. Proceedings and reports for year ending September 30, 1927. 29 p. 8°. (Miss Gertrude C. Mann, secretary, Box 418, Charlottesville, Va.)

205. Johnson, Charles S. [Negro education]. *In his*
Negro in American civilization. New York,
Henry Holt and Co., 1930. p. 224-87.

The author attempts: 1. To give a picture,
based upon facts, of Negro education in the
common schools of the South and North; 2. To
review critically the literature concerning the
educability of the Negro, and to state conclusions
warranted by these data. Summarizes as follows:
1. The final elimination of Negro illiteracy
depends upon improved rural schools and "equali-
zation of educational opportunity among the
various sections of the country." 2. Common
schools for Negroes in the South are usually
inefficient because of unsuitable buildings,
and poor teaching (due to meager salaries paid).
The efficiency of Negro schools coincides with
the ability of States to support education.
3. The rapid influx of southern Negroes into the
North has created a problem whose solution is
taxing the intelligence of the best educational
leadership. 4. The presented data lead to the
conclusion that "the efficiency of Negro children
as measured by achievement tests in the fundamental school subjects is less than that of white
children," but "there is a high correlation between school efficiency and educational efficiency
of pupils. As the efficiency of the school system for Negroes approaches that of the system
for whites, the divergence in achievement ratios
becomes less noticeable. The assumption holds,
at least tentatively, that the inefficiency of
Negro pupils is at least as much a fault of a
poor educational system and an inferior back-
ground, as of an inferior, inherited mental
constitution."

206. Johnson, Charles S. The Negro in American civilization; a study of Negro life and race relations in the light of social research. New
York, H. Holt and company [1930]. xiv, 538 p.
tables. 12°.

207. Johnson, Edwin D. Experimenting with a social
      science project. North Carolina teachers
      record, 2: 70, 77, October 1931.

      The author outlines the teacher-pupil program
      of discipline worked out in the Henderson public
      schools as a unit in the teaching of civics.
      The coordination between the four groups of
      Knights, Safety patrols, Courts, and Social com-
      mittees has made changes too subtle for measure-
      ment, as well as concrete, measurable changes in
      improvement in enrollment and attendance.

208. Johnson, Guy B. The Negro and musical talent.
      Southern workman, 56: 439-44, October 1927.

      A comparison of the Negro with the white race,
      based on studies made by Dr. Carl E. Seashore.

209. Johnson, Guy B. A summary of Negro scores on
      the Seashore music-talent tests. Journal of
      comparative psychology, 11: 383-93, April 1931.

      Tested 3,300 Negroes, compared with results
      found by Seashore. In pitch, Negroes below
      whites except in grade 5. In sense of intensity,
      scores about equal; in grade 5 Negroes superior.
      In sense of time, Negro adults decidedly in-
      ferior, grade 8 not so inferior, grade 5 equals
      whites. In sense of rhythm, Negroes excel,
      grade 5 excels most. In tonal memory, Negroes
      were inferior.

210. Joint committee on Negro child study in New
      York city. A study of delinquent and neglected
      Negro children before the New York city
      children's court, 1925. [New York] Joint com-
      mittee on Negro child study in New York city
      in cooperation with the Department of research
      of the National urban league and the Women's
      city club of New York, 1927. 48 p. 8°.

211. Jones, M. Ashby. Hampton's gift to the South.
     Southern workman (semi-centennial number), 48:
     289-98, June 1919.

     Education of the Negro at Hampton normal and
     agricultural institute, Va.

*   Jones, M. Ashby. See also 171.

212. Jones, Thomas E. Fisk university. Southern
     workman, 56: 9-15, January 1927.

213. Jones, Thomas J. East Africa and education.
     Southern workman, 54: 249-53, June 1925.

214. Jones, Thomas Jesse. Educational adaptations.
     Report of ten years' work of the Phelps-Stokes
     fund, 1910-1920. New York, Phelps-Stokes
     fund, 1920. 92 p. 8°.

215. Jones, Thomas Jesse. Negroes and the census of
     1910. Reprinted from the Southern workman for
     August 1912. [Hampton, Va., 1912]. 16 p.
     8°.

*   Jones, Thomas Jesse. See also 7, 328, 329, 366.

216. Julius Rosenwald fund. Review for the year.
     [by] Edwin R. Embree. Chicago, Ill., The
     Fund, 1931. 38 p.

     Presents the following: The place of universi-
     ties in the Southern renaissance, p. 10-16.
     The year's work--public schools for Negroes, p.
     17-20; Negro health; general education, p. 31;
     social studies, p. 31-34.

K

217. Kellogg, W.N., and Eagleson, B.M. The growth of
social perception in different racial groups.
Journal of educational psychology, 22: 367-75,
May 1931.

Compares the growth of social perception in
Negroes and whites by following G.S. Gates'
procedure in measuring growth in social perception in 458 white children from three to fourteen
years old. Accordingly 332 Negro children (ages
three to fourteen) were tested by means of six
pictures of the Ruckmick series presented one at a
time to each subject, who then attempted to indicate the emotion represented. The only un-
controlled factor in the procedure was the geographical difference of the Negroes and whites.
The study shows that a striking similarity was
evidenced year by year in the data for the two
racial groups.

218. Kenney, John A. How Tuskegee institute is promoting better health conditions in the South.
Modern medicine, 1: 627-30, November 1919. illus.

219. Kenya, Colony and protectorate of. Educational
department. Annual report, 1929. Nairobi,
The Government press, 1930. 23 p.

220. Kidd, A.L. The Florida agricultural and mechanical college. Bulletin (organ of the
National association of teachers in colored
schools), 11: 13-14, 28, April-May 1931.

The writer summarizes the recent developments
at the Florida state college and predicts an even
greater usefulness than has been characteristic in
the past.

*   Kirkland, J.H.   See 171.

221.   Klein, Arthur J., director.   Survey of Land-
       grant colleges and universities.   Washington,
       Government printing office, 1930.   2 v.   8°.
       (U.S. Office of education.   Bulletin, 1930,
       no. 9.)

       Report of the survey of the 69 colleges and
       universities maintained in accordance with the
       provisions of the Morrill act of 1862.   Congress
       provided the funds for this survey which was
       carried on by 80 specialists over a period of
       three years.   Vol. II contains the following:
       Part X, Negro Land-grant colleges.   Each volume
       is indexed and the preface describes the tech-
       niques used in making the survey.

222.   Klineburg, Otto.   The question of Negro intel-
       ligence.   Opportunity, 9: 366-67, December
       1931.

       The writer examines the results of several
       investigations of Negro intelligence.   He is
       led to conclude that "the difference between
       white and Negro children in intelligence-test
       scores tends to disappear as the environments
       of the two groups approach equality."

223.   Knight, Edgar W.   Reconstruction and education
       in South Carolina.   South Atlantic quarterly,
       18: 350-64, October 1919.

       A history of measures relating to public
       schools undertaken by the State government of
       South Carolina during the reconstruction period
       following the Civil War.

224. Knight, Edgar W. Reconstruction and education
in Virginia. [Durham, N.C., 1916]. 36 p.
8°.

Reprinted from South Atlantic quarterly, vol.
15, nos. 1 and 2, January and April 1916.

L

225. La Conférence internationale pour l'enfance
africaine. Revue Internationale de l'Enfant,
12: 221-48, September-October 1931.

The International conference on the African
child held at Geneva, June 22-25, 1931, was the
first of the studies of the non-European child
planned by the organization, U.I.S.E., founded
by Eglantyne Jebb. The participants in the
conference consisted of 233 white persons and
7 Negroes, and included 15 delegates of the
governments belonging to the League of nations
and two Government observers.

226. Lacy, L.D. Relative intelligence of white and
colored children. Elementary school journal,
26: 542-46, March 1926.

Study made in the public schools of Oklahoma
City; data obtained from the regular testing
program which is being carried on in the schools.

227. Landsdown, W.L. Historical sketch of school
and early pioneers of Enid, Okla. Bulletin

(National association of teachers in colored schools), 12: 21-22, 29, December 1931.

Historical development of Booker T. Washington high school in Enid, Okla.

228. Lane, Franklin K. Annual report of the secretary of the interior for the fiscal year ended June 30, 1918. Washington, Government printing office, 1918. 193 p. 8°.

Discusses present conditions and prospects with reference to education as a national concern, education of native-born illiterates, Negroes, and the foreign-born, and Americanization.

229. Lane, Franklin K. Armstrong's contribution to education. Southern workman, 48: 106-12, March 1919.

Address delivered at the Hampton normal and agricultural institute, Hampton, Va., at the celebration of Founder's day, January 26, 1919.

* Lathrop, F.W. See 411.

* Lawrence, W.P. See 25.

230. Leavell, R.H. What does the Negro want? The answer of the Douglass public school. Outlook, 122: 604-606, August 20, 1919.

Tells of the work of the Douglass high school of Cincinnati and how it is meeting the needs of the Negro.

*   Lee, J.R.E. See 277.

231. Leeward Islands. Report on the Education department for the year ended March 31, 1929. An-
tigua, S. Coleridge Carmichael, 1929. 14 p.
Appendices.

232. Leonard, Jacob Calvin. History of Catawba college, formerly located at Newton, now at Salisbury, North Carolina. [Salisbury, N.C., 1927].
352 p. front., plates, ports. 8°.

233. Lewis, F.A. The correlation of an extracurricular
activity with other school subjects--The school
garden. Bulletin (National association of
teachers in colored schools), 10: 7-8, June-
July 1930.

The general purpose of the author is to show
how the keen interest and enthusiasm of pupils
in an extracurricular activity (the garden contest) is made to serve as a pivot about which
work in all of the subjects of the school re-
volve. It is shown how work and material for
the garden contest are correlated with arithmetic, English, geography, history, civics,
reading, spelling, penmanship, music, nature-
study, health work, drawing, domestic art, and
manual training.

*   Lichtenberger, J.P. See 10.

234. Locke, Alain, comp. A decade of Negro self-expression. Compiled by Alain Locke, with a
foreword by Howard W. Odum. Charlottesville,
Va., Michie company, printers, 1928. 20 [1]
p. 8°. (The trustees of the John F. Slater
fund. Occasional papers no. 26.)

235. Locke, Alain. Negro education bids for par.
Survey, 54: 567-70, 592-93, September 1, 1925.

This issue is the education number of Survey.

236. Locke, Alain Le Roy. Oxford contrasts. Independent, 67: 139-42, July 15, 1909.

237. Loram, Charles T. The education of the South
African native. London, New York [etc.],
Longmans, Green, and co., 1917. xx, 340 p.
12°.

Writer is an inspector of schools in Natal,
and was formerly a fellow in education at
Teachers college, Columbia university. During
his stay in the United States, he made a direct
study of various Negro schools in the South,
and incorporates the results of his investigations in this book for their bearing on the
African work.

238. Louisville, Ky. Board of education. Bureau of
research. Partial report on a study of Negro
education in Louisville, Kentucky. Louisville,
Ky., Board of education, 1931. 23+3, ms.

The study is being undertaken with a view to
determine how the schools are meeting the vocational needs of the colored students of Louisville. Results indicate that too many students
plan to enter professions; those students com-
pleting higher education enter more skilled
professions; occupations of Negroes of Louisville
indicate that unskilled work is major field open
to Negroes; where trades are taught exclusively
to Negroes, the schools find difficulty in
placing graduates; vocational subjects taught
in Louisville high schools prepare students for

normal home situations rather than for specific
vocations (with exceptions of teacher preparation
work and commercial work).

*   Lovelady, Bert E. See 144.

239. Lyford, Carrie Alberta. A Hampton girl's training. Southern workman, 49: 209-16, May 1920.
illus.

240. Lyford, Carrie A. Home economics for Negro girls.
Southern workman, 50: 513-18, November 1921.

Discusses the purpose of home-economics training; the planning for courses; preparation of
teachers, etc.

241. Lyford, Carrie Alberta. Homemaking needs based
on location and nationality--needs of the
Negro. Vocational education magazine, 1: 113-
16, October 1922.

Mc

242. McAllister, Jane Ellen. Training of Negro teachers in Louisiana. New York, Teachers college,
Columbia university, 1929. 95 p. 8°. (Teachers college. Contributions to education, no.
364.)

Bibliography.

243. McCormick, William B. Catholic education in
     Haiti. America, 26: 223-24, December 24,
     1921.

244. McCuistion, Fred. Financing schools in the South.
     1930. Nashville, Tenn., State directors of
     educational research in the southern states,
     1930. 29 p.

     This pamphlet includes data regarding sources,
     amounts, and distribution of public school
     revenue in the southern states for 1930. It
     is largely a discussion of the data presented
     in seven tables and graphs. The titles of the
     tables are: Actual and assessed wealth for all
     public elementary and high schools in southern
     states, 1929-1930; income for all public elemen-
     tary and high schools in southern states, 1929-
     1930; sources and amounts of public school
     revenues in 15 southern states, 1929-1930;
     public school enrollment and current expenditures
     in 14 southern states, 1929-1930; summary of
     expenditures in colored schools; ability to edu-
     cate; and effort, or willingness to educate.
     There is a spot map showing the percentage of
     current expenditure received by Negroes in cer-
     tain states.

245. McCuistion, Fred. The South's Negro teaching
     force. Nashville, Tenn., Julius Rosenwald
     Fund, 1931. 29 p.

     The purpose of the study as stated by the
     author is "to present a brief summary of
     available data regarding the Negro teaching
     force of the South, and to discuss problems con-
     nected with the training and distribution of
     these teachers in Southern States." Teacher-
     training institutions are discussed under the
     following subjects: Number and type, amounts

invested, annual budgets, and expenditures. The
following topics serve as headings for the discussion of the teaching force: Number of teaching
positions, number of certified teachers, increases,
annual demands, number in training, number com-
pleting training courses last year, training
levels of present force, improvement of teachers-
in-service, salaries, teaching load, teaching
equipment, and graduate work. Among other things
the report concludes that 38 per cent of the
South's Negro teaching force have less than high
school training; and 58 per cent have less than
two years beyond high school. The typical rural
Negro teacher is a woman about 27 years of age,
has completed high school, and had ten weeks of
summer school. She teaches 47 children through
six grades for a term of six months, receiving
an annual salary of $360.00. In 1912 the pupil-
teacher ratio was 67.

In 1930 there were 47,426 certified teachers
in 15 southern states with an annual requirement
of 6,310 new teachers. Fourteen thousand and
seventy-two students were enrolled in teacher-
training institutions. It is suggested that a
capital outlay of $28,363,780 and an annual
operating budget of $4,640,000 are needed for
the training of Negro teachers. In discussing
teaching equipment in nine southern states for
1928, the study reports white enrollment, which
constituted 69 per cent of the total, received
91 per cent of all funds expended, while the
31 per cent colored enrollment received only 9
per cent of the expenditures. The author suggests the following problems for further study:
1. What is the present practice with regard to
certification of the Negro teachers? 2. What
would be the desirability, results, and cost of
a minimum salary schedule for colored teachers
in the various states? 3. What factors determine
Negro teachers' salaries? 4. What are the factors
of increased cost under a dual system of education? 5. How does pupil progress in colored
schools compare with progress in white schools?

6. How are pupils distributed according to age
and grade? 7. What do Negro high-school and
college graduates do after leaving school?
8. How much property do Negroes own and what
do they contribute toward the cost of education?

246. McDavid, Mary Foster. Ways by which illiterate
adults are taught. Southern workman, 61: 82-
87, February 1932.

A description of the opportunity schools for
Negro adults of Alabama with illustrations of
textbook materials, desk work, informal tests,
and supplementary work.

247. McDougald, Gertrude E. Vocational guidance for
Negro children. Southern workman, 51: 359-62,
August 1922.

Work of public schools of New York city
described. Vocational training and guidance
of Negroes.

*   Macgregor, J.K. See 436.

248. McGrew, J.H. Y.M.C.A. work for Virginia Negroes.
Southern workman, 46: 237-40, April 1917.

249. McKenzie, F.A. Negro health education. Fisk
university news, 9: 26-31, June 1919.

Reprinted from the May issue of the Journal
of the outdoor life.
A paper read before the Southern tuberculosis
conference, Birmingham, Ala., January 23, 1919.

M

250. Mack, Lillian C. The Jeanes conference. Southern workman, 61: 37-42, January 1932.

   The author describes a conference of Jeanes supervisors and workers which was held at Tuskegee institute, October, 1931. The writer feels that this was a vital and significant conference both for education in general and for the cause of the half million under-privileged children whom these Jeanes supervisors serve.

251. Magic yeast of Tuskegee. Literary digest, 109: 23, May 9, 1931.

   The spirit of the work of Booker T. Washington has been the "magic yeast" which has aided both racial groups in America by systematizing industrial education.

252. Maltby, Frances. The movable school. Survey, 45: 888-89, March 19, 1921.

   Work among Negro farmers in Madison county, Ala., described. The U.S. Department of agriculture, in cooperation with the Agricultural and home economics extension work of the Alabama polytechnic institute, has been making an extensive campaign among the Negroes of rural communities in the South through the medium of the movable school.

*   Maltby, R.D. See 411.

253. Manly, A.L. Vocational guidance for colored people. Vocational guidance magazine, 4: 79-82, November 1925.

254. Marcais, William. La langue arabe dans l'Afrique du Nord. L'Enseignement public, 105: 20-39, Janvier 1931.

A careful discussion of the use of the Arabic language in North Africa. The first of a series.

255. Markoe, William M. Negro higher education. America, 26: 558-60, April 1, 1922.

256. Martha Schofield and Negro education. Southern workman, 60: 150-51, April 1931.

A description of the work of Martha Schofield, founder of Schofield school, Aiken, S.C.

257. Mason, Mary L. Illiteracy--the Negro's fight to wipe it out. American teacher, 11: 14-16, May 1927.

258. Mauritius colony. Annual report on primary education. 1928.

259. Mays, B.E. After college, what? for the Negro. Crisis, 37: 408-10, December 1930.

The author endeavored to find what is being done in Negro high schools and colleges to aid Negro students in an intelligent choice of occupation. The results of this study show that practically nothing is being done.

260. Mehus, O.M. Education and racial adjustment.
     High school teacher, 8: 11-12, January 1932.

     Reports briefly the Conference on dual educa-
     tion held at George Peabody college, Nashville,
     Tenn., July 20-23, 1931. This conference was
     financed by the Carnegie corporation. Discussions
     were held on contributions made by southern col-
     leges to improved race relationships by courses
     offered or investigations made, equalization of
     educational opportunity, and the need of an ob-
     jective attitude.

*   Meserve, C.F. See 366.

261. Methodist Episcopal Church. Board of education.
     Proceedings ... of the annual meeting, June
     17-19, 1931. [Chicago, Ill., The Board, 1931].
     p. 292-361. (Rev. William S. Bovard, 740 Rush
     Street, Chicago, Ill., secretary.)

     Contains: 4. Thomas Nicholson: Report ... on
     better schools for Negroes, p. 329-333.

262. Middlemiss, H.S., ed. Narcotic education.
     Edited report of the proceedings of the first
     World conference on narcotic education, Phila-
     delphia, Pennsylvania, July 5, 6, 7, 8, and 9,
     1926. Washington, D.C., H.S. Middlemiss,
     Columbian Building, 1926. 403 p. 8°.

     Contains: 4. Miguel A. Branley: Narcotic edu-
     cation in Cuba--its accomplishments, p. 268-72.

263. Miller, Kelly. Education of the Negro in the
     North. Educational review, 62: 232-38, Octo-
     ber 1921.

264. Miller, Kelly. Forty years of Negro education.
      Educational review, 36: 484-98, December 1908.

265. Miller, Kelly. The higher education of the Negro
         is at the crossroads. Educational review, 72:
         272-78, December 1926.

      The writer says that experience is demonstrating
      that for the present the wise method of adminis-
      tration of higher institutions for Negroes is
      where the whites of the highest character,
      standing, and connection form the dominant ele-
      ment in the governing boards with a Negro staff
      in immediate charge of intimate administration
      and instruction. This is the method of Tuskegee,
      Morehouse, Biddle, Clark, and many schools under
      denominational control.

266. Miller, Kelly. National responsibility for the
         education of the Negro. Educational review,
         58: 31-38, June 1919.

      Discusses the inadequacy of provisions made for
      Negro education. Advocates the higher education.
      Paper read before the Department of superinten-
      dence, March 1, 1918.

267. Miller, Kelly. The practical value of the higher
         education of the Negro. Education, 36: 234-40,
         December 1915.

      Says that the chief aim of the higher educa-
      tion is to produce an efficient leadership. The
      writer states that owing to the fact that the
      Negro is confined to "a separate social area,"
      it becomes necessary that his needs should be
      met by the professional class of his own race.

*   Miller, Kelly. See also 280.

268. Mitchell, Ida, and others. A study of association in Negro children. Psychological review,
26: 354-59, September 1919.

Study consists of 300 association test records,
the subjects being Negro children of New York
city schools, in age groups of 25 ranging from
14 to 15 years, and about equally divided as to
sex. Says that Negro children, on the whole,
show "further departure than white ones from
the normal adult associational standard."

269. Montoro, Rafael. Popular education. Inter-
America, 2: 79-81, December 1918.

Problem of popular education in Cuba.

270. Moroney, T.B. The Americanization of the Negro.
Catholic world, 113: 577-84, August 1921.

Shows the work that the Catholics have been
and are doing for the education of Negroes.

271. Moroney, T.B. Catholic educational effort for
the Negroes. Catholic educational review,
18: 511-23, November 1920.

272. Morse, Josiah. A comparison of white and colored
children measured by the Binet scale of intelligence. Popular science monthly, 84: 75-
79, January 1914.

Measurement with the Binet scale, as revised
by Dr. H.H. Goddard. Tests made by Alice C.
Strong on white and colored school children of
Columbia, S.C. Concludes that "negro children
from 6 to 12 and possibly 15 years are mentally
different, and also younger than southern white
children of corresponding age, and this condition

is partly due, at least, to causes that are native or racial."

273. Morton-Finney, J. Negro educators for Negro education. School and society, 24: 225-29, November 20, 1926.

Some opinions founded on recent Fisk and Howard university incidents.

274. Moten, Robert R. A life of achievement--Booker T. Washington. Southern workman, 45: 177-82, March 1916.

*   Moton, Robert R. See also 171.

275. Murray, A. Victor. The school in the bush: a critical study of the theory and practice of native education in Africa. London, New York, Longmans, Green and co., 1929. xx, 413 p. 12°.

276. Mustard, H.S., and Waring, J.L. Heights and weights of colored school children. American journal of public health, 16: 1017-22, October 1926.

Comparison made between white and colored school children in Rutherford county, Tenn.

N

277. National association of teachers in colored
schools. Proceedings of the eighth annual
session ... held in St. Louis, Missouri,
July 26-30, 1911. [Hampton, Va.] Press of
the Hampton institute, 1912. 36 p. 8°.
(J.R.E. Lee, secretary, Tuskegee institute,
Ala.)

Contains: W.T.B. Williams: The outlook in
Negro education, p. 12-30. (Also in Southern
workman, 40: 638-52, November 1911.)

278. National education association. Addresses and
proceedings of the fifty-ninth annual meeting
held at Des Moines, Iowa, July 3-8, 1921.
Pub. by the Association, Secretary's office,
Washington, D.C., 1921. 823 p. 8°. (J.W.
Crabtree, secretary, 1201 Sixteenth Street,
N.W., Washington, D.C.)

Contains: *Department of rural education.*--(Atlantic City meeting). 37. J.H. Dillard: The Negro
in rural education and country life, p. 580-83.

279. National education association. Department of
superintendence. Proceedings ... at the annual
meeting held at Detroit, Mich., February 21-26,
1916. Published by the Association, 1916.
220 p. 8°.

Contains: 7. O.T. Corson: Booker T. Washington
--an appreciation, p. 93-98.

280. National education association. Department of
     superintendence. Atlantic City meeting, Feb-
     ruary 25-March 2, 1918. Journal of the
     National education association, 2: 649-744,
     May 1918.

     Contains: 8. National responsibility for edu-
     cation of the colored people--A. The status of
     Negro education [by] Kelly Miller, p. 731-34.--
     B. The nation's responsibility to the South for
     Negro education [by] W.T.B. Williams, p. 734-38.--
     C. The nation's responsibility to itself for
     Negro education and its constitutional power to
     render aid thereto [by] Isaac Fisher, p. 738-42;
     Discussion, p. 742-44. 9. F.I. Cooper: Stan-
     dardization of schoolhouse planning and construc-
     tion, p. 745-52.

281. National education association of the United
     States. Addresses and proceedings of the fifty-
     fourth annual meeting held at New York City,
     July 1-8, 1916. Ann Arbor, Mich., Pub. by
     the Association, 1916. 1112 p. 8°.

     General sessions.--Contains: 14. H.B. Frissell:
     The education of the Negro, p. 106-11.

282. National education association of the United
     States. Journal of proceedings and addresses
     of the forty-sixth annual meeting, held at
     Cleveland, Ohio, June 29-July 3, 1908. Winona,
     Minn., the Association, 1908. xii, 1251 p.
     8°. (Irwin Shepard, secretary, Winona, Minn.)

     Contains: 5. B.T. Washington--Negro education
     and the nation, p. 87-93.

283. National education association of the United
     States. Proceedings of the sixty-seventh
     annual meeting, held at Atlanta, Georgia,

June 28–July 4, 1929. vol. 67. Washington,
D.C., The National education association,
1201 Sixteenth street, NW., 1929. 1215 p.
8°.

Department of rural education.--38. Leo M. Favrot: Negro education in the South--abstract,
p. 472-77.

284. National league of nursing education. Proceedings of the thirtieth annual convention ...
held at Detroit, Michigan, June 16 to June 21,
1924. Baltimore, Williams & Wilkins company,
1925. 266 p. 8°. (Ada Belle McCleery, secretary, Evanston Hospital, Evanston, Ill.)

Contains: 8. Report of the Committee on training schools for Negro nurses, p. 214.

285. The Negro common school, Georgia. Crisis, 32:
248-64, September 1926. tables. diagrs.

Gives the history, laws, expenditures, etc.,
regarding Negro education in Georgia, to be
followed by studies in other southern states.

286. The Negro common school, Mississippi. Crisis,
33: 90-102, December 1926. illus.

The second of the reports of the Garland fund
investigation series, the first appearing in the
September number of The Crisis. The third of
the series will appear in the February 1927 issue, entitled "The Negro common school, North
Carolina."

287. Negro education. A study of the private and
higher schools for colored people in the United
States. Prepared in cooperation with the

Phelps-Stokes fund under the direction of Thomas Jesse Jones. In two volumes. Illustrated. Washington, 1917. (Bulletin, 1916, no. 38, 39.)

288. Negro education in North Carolina. School and society, 14: 53, July 30, 1921.

The State department of education of North Carolina has created a division of Negro education, with an enlarged staff of white and Negro assistants.

288A. Negro public schools. Independent, 73: 217-19, July 25, 1912.

289. Negro teachers' association and school improvement league of Virginia. Annual report.... Norfolk, February 27-28, 1913. 44 p. 8°. (A.E. Tucker, secretary.)

290. Negro year book; an annual encyclopedia of the Negro, 1921-1922, ed. by Monroe N. Work. Tuskegee institute, Ala., Negro year book company, 1922. vii, 495 p. 8°.

Education, educational funds, universities, colleges, schools, and libraries, with statistics, etc., p. 229-84.

291. Neville, H.O. Education in the island of Cuba. Bulletin of the Pan American union, 56: 563-76, June 1923. illus.

This is an historical sketch of the development of education in Cuba.

292. New buildings at Atlanta university. School and
     society, 34: 693, November 21, 1931.

     News item on the $1,000,000 anonymous donation
     to Atlanta university for constructing new
     buildings.

293. New Jersey state teachers' association. Annual
     report and proceedings of the 66th annual
     meeting ... Atlantic City, N.J., December 28-
     30, 1920. Camden, N.J., Sinnickson Chew &
     sons co., 1921. 247 p. 8°. (H.J. Neal, sec-
     retary, Collingswood, N.J.)

     Contains: 2. J.R.P. Brock: Work of the colored
     schools, p. 43-47.

294. Newbold, N.C. Educational accomplishments and
     challenges in North Carolina. Southern work-
     man, 61: 10-16, January 1932.

     Reports progress made in education for Negroes
     in North Carolina during the past ten years,
     including the accreditment of the five institu-
     tions for higher learning, the accreditment of
     104 high schools, increase in number of class-
     rooms, and the higher level attained in teacher
     preparation. The challenge presented suggests
     that Negro parents can help the situation by
     causing increased daily attendance, acquainting
     themselves with school laws, and actively co-
     operating with the school officials in a program
     designed for continued advancement.

295. Newbold, N.C. Has North Carolina made any
     progress in Negro education? North Carolina
     teachers' record, 2: 3-4, January 1931.

     "The purpose in view is to point out that a
     state-wide program is in progress of development,

that the State's leadership, white and black, is
working together intelligently, courageously,
and faithfully, toward higher and still higher
goals of accomplishment, and that reasonably
steady and satisfying progress is being made."

296. Newbold, N.C. Negro education in North Carolina.
     Journal of rural education, 4: 145-56, December
     1924.

     Discusses the progress made within the past
     four years in this state.

297. Newbold, N.C. North Carolina's adventure in
     good will. High school journal, 13: 119-23,
     March 1930.

298. Newbold, N.C. Unfinished tasks and new oppor-
     tunities in education in North Carolina. North
     Carolina teachers record, 2: 66-67, 75-76,
     October 1931.

     The unfinished tasks are: 1. Jeanes supervisors
     in counties that need them and where none are
     at work now; 2. high-school opportunities for
     Negro children where such do not exist; 3. new
     and larger school buildings with adequate equip-
     ment for Negro children throughout the state.
     The new opportunities are stated as: 1. Long-term
     summer schools, or special winter terms for
     ministers; 2. opportunity for development of
     dramatic art in high schools and colleges; and
     3. productive scholarship.

299. Newbold, N.C. The White House conference. Its
     significance to the National association of
     teachers in colored schools. Bulletin (National
     association of teachers in colored schools),
     12: 19-20, October 1931.

The writer, through quotations from the report
of the subcommittee of the White House conference
on Negro schools, shows the need for participa-
tion on the part of the Association in plans for
the promotion of a health program for Negro
children. He suggests that through committee
appointments or otherwise the association engage
(1) in the needed extension of public-health
service; (2) in assisting institutions of higher
learning toward adoption of adequate health-
education programs, especially for the training
of teachers; (3) in organizing programs for the
study of local health conditions; (4) in setting
up at least one health council in every county
and large community in the South.

*   Nicholson, Thomas. See 261.

300.   Nigeria. Annual report on the Education depart-
       ments, northern and southern provinces, for
       the year 1929. Lagos, Government printer,
       1930. 70 p.

301.   Noble, Stuart Grayson. Educational values in
       schools for Negroes. South Atlantic quarterly,
       18: 116-24, April 1919.

       Claims that the education furnished for the
       Negro in the past has not functioned to any con-
       siderable extent in social efficiency. A cur-
       riculum based on economic efficiency, morality,
       sociability, and health should be productive of
       good results.

302.   Noble, Stuart Grayson. Forty years of the public
       schools in Mississippi, with special reference
       to the education of the Negro. New York,
       Teachers college, Columbia university, 1918.

142 p. tables, diagrs. 8°. (Teachers college, Columbia university. Contributions to education, no. 94.)

Bibliography: p. 137-38.

303. Northern Rhodesia Government. Annual report of the Director of European education for the year 1929. 21 p.

O

*   Odum, H.W. See 10, 234.

303A. Oldham, J.H. Hollis B. Frissell and Hampton. Constructive quarterly, 6: 569-76, September 1918.

*   Oldham, J.H. See also 55A.

304. Oosthuizen, P.J. Efficiency of the Vineland adjustment score card for measuring social behavior. Journal of educational research, 33: 280-87, April 1931.

This article reports the results of an investigation, carried on in a South African school, to test the efficacy of a method purporting to measure quantitatively the social behavior of an individual in relation to his environment.

305. Ottermann, Charles. A unique Negro school. Southern workman, 53: 213-19, May 1924.

Describes the work of the Harriet Beecher Stowe school of Cincinnati, Ohio.

* Ousley, C.N. See 367.

306. Ovington, Mary White. Closing the little black schoolhouse: second National Negro conference results in new organization. Survey, 24: 343-45, May 28, 1910.

307. Oxley, Lawrence A. North Carolina and her crippled Negro children. Southern workman, 50: 74-78, February 1931.

The article includes an account of the progress which has been made in obtaining hospital facilities in North Carolina for those crippled Negro children who need orthopedic treatment and hospitalization.

P

308. Park, R.E. Agricultural extension among the Negroes. World to-day, 15: 820-26, August 1908.

* Parks, P.C. See 165.

309. Patrick, James Ruey. A study of ideals, intelligence and achievements of Negroes and

whites. [Athens, Ga., 1926]. 48 p. tables.
8°. (On cover: Bulletin of the University of
Georgia, vol. 27, no. 1, December 1926.)

Phelps-Stokes fellowship studies no. 8.
Thesis (M.A.)--University of Georgia, 1926.

310. Peabody, Francis G. Education for life. Southern
workman, 55: 248-56, June 1926.

Address delivered at Tuskegee institute, April
1926, with special bearing on Negro education.

311. Peabody, Francis Greenwood. Education for life;
the story of Hampton institute, told in con-
nection with the fiftieth anniversary of the
foundation of the school. Garden City, N.Y.,
Doubleday, Page & company, 1918. 303 p.
front., illus. 8°.

Bibliography: p. 329-34.

* Peabody, Francis Greenwood. See also 188.

312. Peabody, G.F. For Negro education. Southern
workman, 59: 109-10, March 1930.

* Pearson, James H. See 411.

313. Pechstein, L.A. The problem of Negro education
in northern and border cities. Elementary
school journal, 30: 192-99, November 1929.

314. Pendleton, Helen B. Education for social work
among Negroes in the South. Southern workman,
56: 71-77, February 1927.

Describes work of the Houston, Tex., Social
service bureau.

315. Perterras, P. Education of African natives.
Westminster, 170: 643-48, December 1908.

316. Peterson, Joseph. The comparative abilities of
white and Negro children. Baltimore, Williams
& Wilkins company, 1923. 141 p. tables,
diagrs. 8°. (Comparative psychology monographs,
ed. by W.S. Hunter. vol. 1, serial no. 5,
July 1923.)

317. Phillips, Byron A. The Binet tests applied to
colored children. Psychological clinic, 8:
190-96, December 15, 1914.

In summarizing, the author says that "the
colored children are retarded to a much greater
extent both pedagogically and psychologically
than the white children; and secondly, that the
white children are accelerated to a much greater
extent than the colored children."

* Phillips, J.H. See 366, 367.

318. Pi lambda theta, Alpha gamma chapter (Boston
university). A study in prejudice. Pi lambda
theta journal, 11: 7-15, December 1931.

A summary of an extensive study of racial,
religious, and national prejudices. Contains
an excellent bibliography.

319. Not used.

320. Pratt, K.C. A note upon the relation of activity to sex and race in young infants. Journal of social psychology, 3: 118-20, February 1932.

Stabilimeter records of white and Negro infants show "that sex and race are negligible factors in the general bodily activity of the new-born child."

321. President Hoover's address at the Tuskegee institute. School and society, 33: 571-72, April 25, 1931.

The President's address commemorating the fiftieth anniversary of the founding of Tuskegee institute. "The greatest single factor in the progress of the Negro race has been the schools, private and public, established and conducted by high-minded, self-sacrificing men and women of both races and all sections of our country, maintained by the states and by private philanthropy, covering the whole field of education from primary school through to college and university."

322. The problem of national education in Cuba. American review of reviews, 63: 208-9, February 1921.

Says that the educational system installed by the United States and turned over to Cuba in 1902 has greatly deteriorated. Gives the reasons assigned for this deterioration by Dr. Arturo Montori, also defects found in the private school system by Dr. Ismael Clark and a committee of four.

323. Pulsifer, Harold T. Practical chivalry. Outlook, 116: 362-63, July 4, 1917.

Development of public school system for Negroes in the South.

324. Purcell, Blanche W. Home economics at Hampton institute. Southern workman, 54: 9-15, January 1925.

Q

325. Quigley, Thomas H. Vocational education in industries. Southern workman, 52: 138-42, March 1923.

Discusses the problem of establishing industrial education for colored youth by the State authorities, in cooperation with the Federal board for vocational education.

R

*   Ramsey, D.H. See 25.

326. Ransom, Reverdy C. Educational problems. Southern workman, 50: 417-20, September 1921.

Excerpts from an address before a union meeting of preachers, farmers, and teachers in conference week at Hampton institute, June 1921.

327. Recent progress in Negro education; by Thomas
Jesse Jones. Washington, 1919. 16 p. (Bulletin, 1919, no. 27.)

Advance sheets from the Biennial survey of education in the United States, 1916-1918.

328. Report of the Commissioner of education for the
year ended June 30, 1912. v. 1-2. Washington,
Government printing office, 1913. 8°.

Volume 1: 7. T.J. Jones: Recent movements in
Negro education, p. 243-56.

329. Report of the Commissioner of education for the
year ended June 30, 1914. Vol. 1. Washington,
Government printing office, 1915. 810 p. 8°.

Contents: 19. T.J. Jones: Negro education,
p. 417-24.

330. Report on standards for Negro schools and colleges. High school quarterly, 18: 80-81,
January 1930.

331. Revista de instruccion publica, publicacion
mensual, organo oficial de la Secretaria de
instruccion publica y bellas artes. Año I,
no. 1 extra. October 1925. Habana, Cuba,
R. Veloso y Cía., Libreria "Cervantes," Av. de
Italia 62. 499 p. plates, tables, diagrs.
8°.

Special volume describing following branches
of education: Primary, secondary, private,
higher, professional, education of women, kindergarten, home economics, national library,
school of arts and trades of Havana, physical
education, etc.

332. Richardson, Clement. Examining the near il-
     literate. Southern workman, 45: 546-50,
     October 1916.

     Negro education in the South.

333. Richardson, Clement. A Rosenwald rural school.
     Southern workman, 45: 17-24, January 1916.

     Describes the Uchee Valley school for Negroes,
     in Russell county, Alabama. Illustrated.

334. Richardson, E.S. The Jeanes supervising teacher--
     a potent force in Negro education. Nation's
     schools, 5: 24-31, April 1930. illus.

     Discusses the part that the Jeanes fund plays
     in the education of Negroes in the South, and
     the work of the supervising teacher in particular.

335. Robinson, W.A. The present status of high-
     school education among Negroes--a factual and
     critical survey. Bulletin (National associa-
     tion of teachers in colored schools), 11:
     3-9, November 1930.

     The author makes a critical survey of high-
     school education among Negroes. The lack of
     facilities ordinarily taken for granted is con-
     sidered; also the training and incentives of-
     fered teachers; and the status of the principal.
     The author ranks the various states from which
     information was received as to teachers'
     salaries, libraries, industrial and vocational
     training facilities, health facilities and
     supervision, and provision for cultural ex-
     periences.

336. Roeckel, P. L'éducation sociale des races
     noires. Paris, V. Giard & E. Brière, 1911.
     296 p. 12°. (Encyclopédie internationale
     d'assistance, prévoyance, hygiène sociale et
     démographie, directeur: Dr. A. Marie. "Démo-
     graphie" III.)

*   Roosevelt, Theodore. See 25.

337. Ross, Mary. The leaven and the loaf. Survey,
     62: 171-75, 212-18, May 1, 1929.

     Describes the work of the Clarke county train-
     ing school, near Athens, Ga., which is one of
     the schools for Negroes aided by the Rosenwald
     fund.

*   Ross, W.A. See 411.

338. Russell, Alexander. Current developments in
     music. Princeton alumni weekly, 27: 539-42,
     February 11, 1927.

     With comment upon the jazz mania, motion pic-
     ture, radio, and the uses of each.

S

*   Sadler, Sir Michael. See 55A.

339. Saint Lucia. Annual report of the inspector of
     schools on the education department, 1928.
     Castries, The Government printer, 1929. 26 p.

340. Saint Vincent. Report on the elementary schools
     for the year 1928-1929. Kingstown, Government
     printer, 1929. 22 p.

341. Sala y Cantos, Angela. Instinto del juego en el
     niño. Investigaciones realizadas en el niño
     cubano. Revista de la facultad de letras y
     ciencias, Universidad de la Habana, 27: 27-98,
     July-October 1918.

     Thesis for the degree of doctor of pedagogy in
     the University of Havana, specially recommended
     for publication by the examining tribunal.

342. Savage, W. Sherman. Legal provisions for Negro
     schools in Missouri from 1865 to 1890. Journal
     of Negro history, 16: 12, July 1931.

     In this study the author reviews the legal pro-
     visions for Negro education in Missouri from
     1865, the date of the passing of the initial law
     to the law in 1889 which stated that separate
     free schools shall be established for the educa-
     tion of children of African descent, and it
     shall hereafter be unlawful in the public schools
     of this state for any colored child to attend a
     white school or any white child to attend a
     colored school, which in effect has virtually
     prohibited the education of Negroes in the
     sparsely settled communities.

343. Savoy, A. Kiger. Garrison demonstration school.
     Bulletin (National association of teachers in
     colored schools), 10: 16-17, June-July 1930.

     A description of the work of the Garrison
     demonstration school of Washington, D.C., show-
     ing how the school carries out its purpose, viz.,
     "to exemplify through classroom work, principles,
     methods, and procedures which have passed the

experimental stage and which have received the
approval of the school administration."

344. Scott, A.S. Effect of familiarity with standardized intelligence tests on subsequent
scores. Bulletin (National association of
teachers in colored schools), 12: 12, December
1931.

Reports a study made in the Negro high school
in Daytona, Fla., designed to investigate the
effect of a testing program on intelligence
tests results.

345. Scott, Emmett J. Brightening up the rural
South. Outlook, 199: 412-14, July 10, 1918.

Details the success of Negro rural schools,
established under the provisions of the Rosenwald
fund.

346. Scott, Emmett. Leisure time and the colored
citizen. Playground, 18: 593-96, January
1925.

347. Scott, Emmett J. "A Negro out of the ordinary."
Southern workman, 44: 98-104, February 1915.

Remarkable career and educational abilities
of Dr. Isaac Fisher, who has "not a drop of
Caucasian blood in his veins." Winner of many
prize essays on scientific, social, and educational subjects.

348. Scott, Emmett J., and Stowe, Lyman Beecher.
Booker T. Washington; builder of a civilization
Garden City, N.Y., Doubleday, Page & company,
1916. 331 p. illus. 8°.

349. Scruggs, Sherman P. Improving reading ability
     in grades V and VI by extensive reading.
     University of Kansas Bulletin of education, 3:
     7, April 1931.

     An experimental study restricted to colored
     children, conducted in a Kansas City, Kans.,
     school system, over a period of 16 weeks. In
     two Negro schools, 108 pupils in fifth and 96
     in sixth grade formed two groups in each, equated
     chiefly on school record and intelligence tests.
     Frequent library visits, special opportunity
     to browse, and reports on all books read were
     used to stimulate experimental groups to read
     four times as many books as control group. Re-
     sults as measured by gains in three reading
     tests showed marked advantage in both rate and
     comprehension for extensive reading group.
     The study was carefully conducted and data are
     convincing.

350. Seabrook, J.W. Fayetteville State normal school.
     North Carolina teachers record, 2: 28-29, 38-
     39, March 1931.

     Description of Fayetteville normal school and
     its problems and aims.

351. Secondary school reform. Revista de Educacion,
     3: 185-93, November 25, 1931.

     Official orders dated July 1 and September 25,
     1931, require the presence of the teacher of the
     next higher class at final examinations in the
     grade schools; and fix the minimum age for en-
     trance to secondary schools at 12 years.

352. Settle, T.S. Recreation for colored citizens--
     needs and methods. Playground, 18: 597-98,
     612-13, January 1925.

353. Seychelles colony. Annual report on education
     for the year 1929. Government printing office,
     1930. 21 p.

354. Seychelles, Colony. Annual report on education
     for the year 1930. Victoria, Government
     printing office, 1931. 19 p.

     The official report on education in Seychelles.

355. Sherwood, Grace H. The Oblates' hundred and one
     years. New York, The Macmillan company, 1931.
     288 p.

     "The Oblate sisters of Providence is a religious
     society of virgins and widows of color. Their end
     is to consecrate themselves to God in a special
     manner not only to sanctify themselves and there-
     by secure the glory of God, but also to work for
     the Christian education of colored children"--
     thus reads the first rule of the first Negro
     sisterhood in the United States, established in
     Baltimore in 1829 through the efforts of a priest,
     M. Joubert. In addition to detailed description
     of the work of this "motherhouse" the author
     devotes chapters to the establishment and work
     of similar institutions in St. Louis, Mo.,
     Leavenworth, Kans., Cuba, Ridge, Md., and Charles-
     ton, S.C.

356. Sibley, James L. County training schools in Ala-
     bama. Southern workman, 45: 407-12, July 1916.

     Work of the new type of school for Negro youth
     in the South, fostered by the States board in co-
     operation with the public school authorities in
     the counties.

357. Sierra Leone. Annual report of the Education
     department for the year 1928. Freetown, Govern-
     ment printing office, 1929. 31 p.

358. Sierra Leone. Education department. Annual re-
     port ... for the year 1929. Freetown, Govern-
     ment printer, 1931. 32 p.

     The annual official report on education in
     Sierra Leone.

359. Sing, S.N. White man's effort for Negro uplift.
     Arena, 40: 66-72, July 1908.

360. Smith, E.E. North Carolina--first! Bulletin
     (official organ of the National association
     of teachers in colored schools), 11: 13-15,
     January 1931.

     Presents efforts of state of North Carolina to
     promote literacy among Negro citizens within the
     state.

*   Smith, Hale W. See 144.

361. Smith, S.L. Negro public schools in the South.
     Southern workman, 56: 315-24, July 1927.

362. Smith, S.L. Negro public schools in the South.
     Southern workman, 57: 449-61, November 1928.

363. Snavely, Tipton R. The Phelps-Stokes fund at
     the University of Virginia. Southern workman,
     56: 129-35, March 1927.

     Studies of Negro sociology and education.

364. Snyder, Howard. Paradise Negro school. Yale review, 11: 158-69, October 1921.

Describes a Negro rural school in Mississippi.

365. South Dakota educational association. Proceedings of the twenty-seventh annual session held at Lead, November 1-2-3, 1909. Pierre, S.D., The Executive Committee [1909?]. 202 p. 8°. (Nina M. Nash, secretary, Aberdeen, S.D.)

Contains: 6. B.T. Washington: Address, p. 66-68.

366. Southern educational association. Journal of proceedings and addresses of the nineteenth annual session, held at Atlanta, Georgia, December 29-31, 1908. [Chattanooga, Tenn.] The Association [1909]. 736 p. 8°. (William F. Feagin, secretary, Montgomery, Ala.)

Contains: 6. T.J. Jones: Relation of the state to the education of the Negro, p. 116-20. 7. J.H. Phillips: Essential requirements of Negro education, p. 121-29. 8. J.H. Dillard: Negro rural schools, p. 130-35. 9. C.F. Meserve: Results of attempts at the higher education of the Negro of the South, p. 136-44. 47. E.L. Hughes: Supervision of Negro schools, p. 463-69.

367. Southern educational association. Journal of proceedings and addresses of the twenty-second annual meeting, held at Houston, Texas, November 30, December 1, 2, 1911. [Chattanooga, Tenn.] The Association [1912]. 722 p. 8°. (William F. Feagin, secretary, Montgomery, Ala.)

Contains: 12. C.N. Ousley: Education of the southern Negro, p. 151-56. 13. J.H. Dillard:

Negro education in the South, p. 156-58. 14. J.H.
Phillips: The education of the southern Negro,
p. 159-69. 15. W.S. Sutton: The education of
the southern Negro, p. 169-88.

368. Southern educational association. Journal of
proceedings and addresses of the twenty-fourth
annual meeting held at Nashville, Tennessee,
October 30 to November 1, 1913. 372 p. 8°.
(R.A. Clayton, secretary-treasurer, Birmingham,
Ala.)

Contains: 11. J.R. Guy: Right kind of education
for the southern Negro in the city, p. 153-60.
12. Jackson Davis: Practical training in Negro
rural schools, p. 160-68; Discussion, p. 168-75.

369. Southern Rhodesia. Report of the Director of
Education for the year 1929. Salisbury, The
Government printer, 1930. 29 p.

370. Statistics of education of the Negro race, 1925-
1926. By David T. Blose. Washington, U.S.
Government printing office, 1928. 42 p. 8°.
(Bulletin, 1928, no. 19.)

371. Stephenson, Gilbert T. Education and crime
among Negroes. South Atlantic quarterly, 16:
14-20, January 1917.

Writer contends that all the available statistics and the unanimous opinion of those acquainted
with the facts show that education--elementary
or advanced, industrial or literary--diminishes
crime among Negroes.

372. Stoutemyer, J. Howard. Religion and race educa-
      tion. Journal of religious psychology, 7:
      273-324, April 1915.

      A very interesting study of the philosophy
      underlying missionary efforts. Evolution of
      religious ideas.

*   Stowe, Lyman Beecher. See 348.

373. Stowell, Jay S. Methodist adventures in Negro
      education. New York, Cincinnati, The Methodist
      book concern [1922]. 190 p. illus. 12°.

374. Streep, R. A comparison of white and Negro
      children in rhythm and consonance. Journal
      of applied psychology, 15: 53-71, February
      1931.

      Studied 637 white and 678 Negro children.
      Negroes were slightly superior in the two phases
      of musical ability tested, perhaps not a racial
      difference. Used children of grades 3 to 6 in
      New York city, ages 8-12 years, giving Seashore
      tests.
      A review of a master's thesis at Columbia
      university. Author has given 10 bibliographical
      titles, and lists problems for further study.

375. Strong, Alice C. Three hundred fifty white and
      colored children measured by the Binet-Simon
      scale of intelligence: a comparative study.
      Pedagogical seminary, 20: 485-515, December
      1913.

      Bibliography: p. 512-15.
      The children tested were in the public schools
      of Columbia, S.C.

376. Studies of Negro education. Journal of social
forces, 1: 585-91, September 1923.

377. Sudan Government. Annual report of the Education
department, 1929. Khartoum, McCorquodale &
co., ltd., 1930. 99 p. maps.

378. Sudan. [Education department]. Annual report
of the education department, 1930. Khartoum,
McCorquodale & co., ltd., 1931. 74 p.

The official report on education in Sudan for
the year 1930.

379. Sumner, F.C. Mental health statistics of Negro
college freshmen. School and society, 33:
574-76, April 25, 1931. tables.

Reports the results of the administering of
S. Daniel House's Mental hygiene inventory to
203 freshmen at Howard university. The writer
found, (1) the mental health of Negro freshmen
is approximately normal; (2) the Negro is slightly
more psychoneurotic in childhood and slightly
more mentally healthy in maturity; (3) the male
Negro college freshman is slightly less normal
than the female in childhood and more noticeably
supernormal in maturity; (4) the more intelligent
the freshman the less normal in mental health he
was in childhood, and the more intelligent the
freshman the more mentally healthy he is in
maturity.

380. Sumner, F.C. Morale and the Negro college.
Educational review, 73: 168-72, March 1927.

Emphasizes the necessity of thoroughness in
Negro colleges.

381. Sunne, Dagny. A comparative study of white and
     Negro children. Journal of applied psychology,
     1: 71-83, March 1917.

     An investigation of the white and Negro children
     of a school in New Orleans by means of the Binet
     and the Yerkes point scales and other tests.

382. Sunne, Dagne. Comparison of white and Negro
     children in verbal and nonverbal tests. School
     and society, 19: 469-72, April 19, 1924.

383. Supervision of Negro rural schools. Southern
     workman, 41: 219-27, April 1912.

     Papers read at a meeting of Negro state teachers
     and school improvement leagues of Virginia held
     at Lynchburg, February 23, 1912.

384. Survey of Negro colleges and universities. Pre-
     pared in the division of higher education,
     Arthur J. Klein, chief. Washington, United
     States Government printing office, 1929. 964 p.
     8°. (Bulletin, 1928, no. 7.)

385. Sutton, W.S. The contributions of Booker T. Wash-
     ington to the education of the Negro. School
     and society, 4: 457-63, September 23, 1916.

     An address delivered April 19, 1916, in New
     Orleans before the Southern conference for edu-
     cation and industry.

386. Sutton, William Seneca. The education of the
     southern Negro. School journal, 80: 332-37,
     September 1913.

     Brief historical survey and "six principles, or
     planks, in the program" for Negro education.

387. Sutton, William Seneca. The education of the
southern Negro. Austin, Tex., University of
Texas, 1912. 24 p. 8°. (Bulletin of the
University of Texas. no. 221. General ser.
23.)

"References": p. 19-24.

* Sutton, William Seneca. See also 367.

* Swanson, H.B. See 411.

T

388. Taft, William H. Hampton's gift to the nation.
Southern workman (semi-centennial number), 48:
299-302, June 1919.

Work of Hampton institute, Va., in advancing
the educational and moral progress of the Negro
in America.

* Taft, William Howard. See also 171, 188.

389. Talbot, Edith A. Hampton to-day. Southern
workman, 51: 509-21, November 1922.

A description of Hampton normal and industrial
school, Hampton, Va., and its activities. Illustrated.

390. Tanganyika Territory. Annual report of the Education department, 1929. Dar es Salaam, The Government printer [1930]. 56 p.

391. Tanganyika Territory. Education department. Annual report, 1930. Dar es Salaam, The Government printer, 1931. 47 p.

    The regular official report on education in the Territory.

392. Taylor, Ben L. The accredited Negro high schools of North Carolina. School and society, 26: 460-64, October 8, 1927.

393. Taylor, R.R. Tuskegee's mechanical department. Southern workman, 50: 457-68, October 1921.

    Methods of teaching the trades, etc., at Tuskegee institute. Illustrated.

394. Thirkield, Wilbur P. The higher education of the Negro. Religious education, 6: 420-23, December 1911.

    Arguments in favor of higher education of the Negro, as really essential to permanent and effective results in elementary training and to the industrial and civic future of the race.

395. Thompson, Mrs. Vinetta. Vocational guidance for Negro boys. Dunbar news, 3: 1, 5-6, December 16, 1931.

    The purpose of the vocational guidance program in the Frederick Douglass junior high school in Harlem is stated as follows: To instill wholesome character, to improve health conditions, and to

equip boys with tools which will enable them to
compete in the modern scheme of civilization.

396. Thurnwald, Richard. The missionary's concern in
     sociology and psychology. Africa, 4: 418-33,
     October 1931.

     Supplementary to a paper in Africa, vol. IV,
     no. 2, entitled "The missionary as an anthropo-
     logical field-worker." The author stresses the
     importance of studying the social life of the
     tribe or tribes with which one works. The
     article contains warnings that "reliable data
     are far preferable to too much systematization
     of dubious material" and "a clear and ample
     description of the state of affairs is always
     preferable." An unusually strong article.

397. Thwing, Charles F. The university at Cairo.
     Independent, 68: 1389-95, June 23, 1910.

398. Tonga. Department of education. Administration
     report ... for the year 1929. Nukualofa, C.S.
     Summers, 1930. 12 p.

     The official annual report on education in
     the Kingdom of Tonga.

399. Torres, Arturo. The educational system of the
     republic of Cuba. Bulletin of the Pan American
     union, 49: 352-57, September 1919.

     Prepared from data furnished by Dr. Ramiro
     Guerra, professor of education in the Normal
     school of Habana, and information contained in
     the Columbus Memorial library of the Pan American
     union.

400. Transvaal (Colony) Education dept. Correspondence relating to the organisation of higher education in the Transvaal. Presented to both houses of Parliament by command of His Excellency the governor. Pretoria, Printed at the Government printing and stationery office, 1908. 34 p. F°.

Correspondence between the Education department, the colonial secretary and the Transvaal university college.

401. Transvaal (Colony) Education dept. The normal college for men and women students, Sunnyside, Pretoria.... [Pretoria, Printed at the Government printing and stationery office, 1908]. 16 p. 8°.

402. Transvaal. Education department. Report for the year ended December 31, 1930. Pretoria, Government printer, 1931. 172 p.

The annual official descriptive and statistical report of education in Transvaal.

403. Trelles, Carlos M. Primary instruction in Cuba; a comparison between it and that of other countries. Inter-America, 7: 401-43, June 1924.

An address delivered in the Instituto de segunda enseñanza of Matanzas, Cuba, August 28, 1923.

404. Trenholm, H. Councill. Radio address of President Trenholm, Washington, D.C., American education week. Bulletin (National association of

teachers in colored schools), 12: 11, 30, December 1931.

Discusses the professionalization of teachers in colored schools.

405. Trinidad and Tobago. Education. Administration Report of the Director of education for the year 1928. Trinidad, The Government printer, 1929. 31 p.

*   Turner, T.W. See 53.

406. Twining, Cicely. Child-welfare work in Mombasa. Mother and child, 2: 254-55, October 1931.

A descriptive and interesting account.

U

407. Uganda Protectorate. Annual report of the Education department for the year ended 31 December, 1928. Entebbe, The Government printer, 1929. 26 p.

408. U.S. Bureau of education. Report of the Commissioner for the year 1907. v. 1-2. Washington, Government printing office, 1908. 8°.

Contains: 12. Education in Hawaii, Porto Rico, and Cuba, p. 359-69.

409. United States. Bureau of education. Report of
     the Commissioner of education for the year
     ended June 30, 1911. v. 1-2. Washington,
     Government printing office, 1912. 8°.

     Contains: vol. 1, ch. 22, p. 609-17, Report of
     the First Universal races congress, held at Lon-
     don July 26-29, 1911, by Felix Adler.

410. United States. Department of state. Report of
     the United States Commission on education in
     Haiti. Washington, Government printing
     office, 1931. 74 p. (Latin American series
     no. 5. October 1, 1930.)

     A report made to the President of the United
     States by a commission which he appointed to
     inquire into educational conditions in Haiti.
     An unusually interesting study in view of the
     fact that Haiti is one of the three governments
     in the world controlled by Negro people.

411. United States. Federal board for vocational
     education. Progress in agricultural education.
     Agricultural education, 3: 152-64, April 1931.
     illus., diagrs., plates, tables, charts.

     Brief reports by regional federal agents of
     material to be found in more extended form in
     the current annual report of the Federal board
     for vocational education. A.P. Williams, Federal
     agent North Atlantic region: Methods of teaching.
     W.A. Ross, Specialist in agricultural education:
     Subject-matter for instruction in vocational
     agriculture. H.B. Swanson, Specialist in agri-
     cultural education: Teacher-training. R.D. Malt-
     by, Federal agent, Southern region: Supervised
     practice. James H. Pearson, Specialist in agri-
     cultural education: Evening and part-time school.
     F.W. Lathrop, Specialist in agricultural educa-

tion: Studies and investigations. H.O. Sargent,
Federal agent, Southern region: Negro schools.

412. Not used.

413. University commission on southern race questions.
Four open letters from the University commission on race questions to the college men of
the South. [Lexington, Va., 1919]. 8 p. 8°.

Contents.--I. Lynching.--II. Education.--
III. Migration.--IV.--A new reconstruction.

414. University commission on southern race questions.
Minutes [1912-17]. [n.p., 1918?]. 75 p.
plates, ports. 8°.

Secretary of commission: W.M. Hunley, Box 722,
Lexington, Va.

V

415. Vermont state teachers' association. Report of
the sixty-second annual convention, Montpelier,
Vt., October 19, 20, and 21, 1911. St. Albans,
Vt., St. Albans messenger co., 1912. 137 p.
12°. (Amy B. Drake, secretary, St. Johnsbury,
Vt.)

Contains: 2. B.T. Washington: The Negro and
the application of education to life, p. 34-
48.

416. Virginia Education commission. Virginia public
schools. Education commission's report to
the Assembly of Virginia. Survey staff's report to the Education commission. Richmond,
Va., Everett Waddey company, 1919. 400 p.
plates. 8°.

Director of the survey: Dr. Alexander J.
Inglis.
Contents: 13. Negro education in Virginia.

W

* Walker, T.C. See 165.

417. Wanger, Ruth. High-school study of the Negro
and his problems. High school teacher, 8:
104-106, 112, March 1932.

After a pre-test was given to determine attitudes with regard to Negroes in a problems-of-
democracy course in the South Philadelphia high
school for girls, an assignment was made embracing
a study of Negro characteristics, effects of
reconstruction, geographical and social conditions,
economic status, contributions to American life,
and proposed constructive solutions. Quotations
are cited from the examination papers of the
girls indicating extent of changes in viewpoint.

* Ware, E.T. See 10.

418. Washington, Booker T. Education for the man
     behind the plow: Tuskegee institute. Inde-
     pendent, 64: 918-20, April 23, 1908.

419. Washington, Booker T. Fifty years of Negro
     progress. Forum, 55: 269-79, March 1916.

     A statistical study. Discusses educational
     advancement of Negroes, etc.

420. Washington, Booker T. How Denmark has taught
     itself prosperity and happiness. World's
     work, 22: 14486-94, June 1911.

421. Washington, Booker T. Is the Negro having a fair
     chance? Century magazine, 85: 46-55, November
     1912.

     Discusses various phases of the subject. Lays
     emphasis on "the lack of a 'square deal' in
     education," as regards the southern Negro.

422. Washington, Booker T. My larger education; being
     chapters from experience. New York, Doubleday,
     Page & Co., 1911. viii, 313 p. 8°.

423. Washington, Booker T. The Negro and illiteracy.
     Independent, 73: 766-68, October 3, 1912.

     Gives statistics based on the last federal
     census. "The figures, just published, show that
     at the present time 69.5, practically 70 per cent,
     of the colored people of the United States can
     both read and write."

424. Washington, Booker T. A remarkable triple
     alliance: how a Jew is helping the Negro

through the Y.M.C.A. Outlook, 108: 485-92, October 28, 1914.

The philanthropies of Julius Rosenwald. Educational activities of Young Men's Christian association.

425. Washington, Booker T. A university education for Negroes. Independent, 68: 613-18, March 24, 1910.

*   Washington, Booker T. See also, 10, 88, 282, 365, 415.

426. Watson, J.B. Louisiana Negroes are advancing. Southern workman, 57: 224-30, May 1928.

Discusses the evolution of Negro education in Louisiana in the past quarter-century.

427. Wauters, Leon. La protection de l'enfance de race non-Européene: La situation démographique au Congo Belge. Revue internationale de l'enfant, 11: 31-42, Janvier 1931.

Excerpts from a study made by M. Wauters in charge of conferences at the Colonial university of Belgium, to which are added some statistical data.

428. Weatherford, W.D. The amazing progress of the Negro race. Methodist review, 62: 509-21, July 1913.

Contains interesting material on the growth of Negro education and schools.

429. Weatherford, W.D. Negro training in the South. Southern workman, 41: 550-58, October 1912.

*   Weatherford, W.D. See also 65.

430. Wesley, Charles H. Negro labor in the United States 1850-1925: a study in American economic history. New York, Vanguard press [1927]. 343 p. 16°.

431. Wesley, Charles H. The problems of sources and methods in history teaching. School review, 24: 329-41, May 1916.

Writer says the method of many of our high school teachers is "detrimental to the growth of historical perspectives or love of history in immature students." Discusses the equipment of the historical department.

432. Whiting, G.W. The present status of elementary education among Negroes in West Virginia. Bulletin (organ of the National association of teachers in colored schools), 11: 21-22, 26-27, April-May 1931.

After summarizing the topics--Qualification for principals, Supervisory duties of principals, Types of schools, Length of term, Enrollment and attendance of pupils, Equipment, and Salaries and training of teachers--the writer concludes that West Virginia has one of the best outlooks of any state South or North. The observation is made that closer supervision with a good scientific technique, and trained elementary principals with a corps of teachers thoroughly acquainted with the child and his problems, are needed to keep pace with modern developments in elementary education.

433. Whitney, Frederick L. Intelligence levels and
school achievement of the white and colored
races in the United States. Pedagogical
seminary, 30: 69-86, March 1923.

434. Wiegräbe, Paul. A reader in the vernacular for
West Africa. Africa, 4: 435-44, October 1931.

A good discussion of the characteristic reading books for native children. The author states,
"It is well known how this practice [of teaching
English too early in the course] injured not only
the native tongue, but also the foreign language,
and what is yet worse, the capacity for thought."

435. Wilkerson, D.A. The vocational choices of
Virginia high school seniors. Virginia teachers bulletin, 7: 1-6, November 1930. graphs,
tables.

A study to ascertain the diversity and nature
of the vocational choices of high-school seniors
and to note whether differences were evident
between the occupational interests of rural and
urban students. The results show that the larger
percentage of seniors make choices of professions;
that there is greater diversity among rural than
urban boys; that choices of rural and urban girls
show no marked differences.

436. Wilkie, A.W., and Macgregor, J.K. Industrial
training in Africa. International review of
missions (Edinburgh), 3: 742-47, October 1914.

Work of the Calabar mission of the United
free church of Scotland.

437. Willcox, William G. Tuskegee's contribution to
     natural efficiency. Southern workman, 45:
     446-48, August 1916.

438. Willcox, William G. Tuskegee's future. Southern
     workman, 46: 268-72, May 1917.

     Address at celebration of Founder's day, Tus-
     kegee, April 5, 1917.

*   Williams, A.P. See 411.

439. Williams, Charles H. Recreation in the lives of
     young people. Southern workman, 46: 95-100,
     February 1917.

     Excerpts from an address delivered in Roanoke,
     Va., before the Negro organization society of
     Virginia, by the physical director for boys,
     Hampton institute.

440. Williams, Fannie C. Introduction to a civic
     project. Bulletin (National association of
     teachers in colored schools), 10: 5-8, June-
     July 1930.

     The author describes the introduction of a
     civic project in the Valena C. Jones elementary
     school, through outlining the details of: 1. Ob-
     jectives for the year; 2. activity program;
     3. moral training.

441. Williams, Talcot. A "close-up" of Negro educa-
     tion. Independent, 105: 538-39, May 21,
     1921.

     An appreciation of the work of Hampton insti-
     tute, Va.

442. Williams, W.T.B. Duplication of schools for
    Negro youth. [Lynchburg, Va., J.P. Bell
    company] 1914. 22 p. 8°. (Trustees of the
    John F. Slater fund, Occasional papers, no.
    15.)

443. Williams, W.T.B. Educational conditions among
    colored people. Southern workman, 51: 409-12,
    September 1922.

444. Williams, W.T.B. Hampton graduates as teachers.
    Southern workman, 48: 503-507, October 1919.

445. Williams, W.T.B. The opportunity of Negro
    teachers. Southern workman, 49: 400-402,
    September 1920.

    An address delivered at the summer school of
    Hampton institute, July 1920, by the field
    director for the Jeanes and Slater funds.

446. Williams, W.T.B. The Yankee schoolma'am in
    Negro education. Southern workman, 44: 73-
    80, February 1915.

    Debt of the Negro to the teachers who came to
    the South to assist in his moral and mental
    uplift.

*   Williams, W.T.B. See also 25, 164, 165, 166,
    277, 280.

447. Wilson, Butler R. What I saw at Calhoun.
    Southern workman, 61: 17-25, January 1932.

    The writer sought to discover whether the
    lessons taught in the classrooms were being

translated into the homes and habits of the
people in the poorest county in Alabama. In
his opinion the progress made by the community
could be explained by the influence of the per-
sonality of the principal of the Calhoun school,
Miss Charlotte Thorn.

448. Wise, Stephen S. A "statesman-educator."
Southern workman, 43: 132-42, March 1914.

Eulogistic sketch of the career of Samuel C.
Armstrong, founder of Hampton institute, by
Rabbi Wise, of New York. Address delivered on
February 1, 1914, in celebration of Founder's
day.

449. Woodson, Carter G. Early Negro education in
West Virginia. Institute, W. Va., The West
Virginia collegiate institute [1921]. 54 p.
8 diagrs. 8°. (The West Virginia collegiate
institute bulletin, ser. 6, no. 3. December
1921. Studies in social science.)

450. Woodson, Carter G. The education of the Negro
prior to 1861. A history of the education
of the colored people of the United States
from the beginning of slavery to the Civil
war. New York and London, G.P. Putnam's sons,
1915. 454 p. 8°.

Bibliography: p. 399-434.

451. Woofter, T.J. Justice to the Negro in education.
High school quarterly, 6: 218-24, July 1918.

Brief of an address before the Association of
county superintendents, Savannah, Ga., April 27,
1918.
Gives a program of what should be done for Negro
education in our common schools.

452. Work, Monroe N. A bibliography of the Negro in
Africa and America. New York, The H.W. Wilson
company, 1928. xxi, 698 p. 8°.

A select reference bibliography on the Negro
with more than 17,000 entries covering the most
worthwhile publications in different languages
issued before 1928.

453. Work, Monroe N. Education. *In* Negro yearbook,
an annual encyclopedia of the Negro, 1931-32.
Chapter xvii. p. 195-253. Tuskegee institute,
Ala., Negro yearbook publishing company, 1931.

Reports the history, progress, and status of
education for Negroes, giving scholastic and
financial statistics, and lists of high schools
and institutions of higher learning.

454. Work, Monroe N. The status of elementary Negro
education. Bulletin (National association of
teachers in colored schools), 11: 14-18,
November 1930.

An investigation of: 1. The relation of elementary education to Negro education in general;
2. How secondary and higher education of the
Negro has been conditioned by elementary education. Summarizes as follows: "In the present
status of elementary education for Negroes there
is the necessity for the elementary schools to
be raised to the place where their progress will
be commensurate with the progress that is being
made in the secondary schools and colleges.
Otherwise, the schools for secondary and higher
training will have to continue to devote a great
part of their effort to doing elementary work."
A plea is made for a just and equitable division
of school funds for the support of Negro schools.

455. Work, Monroe N. Teachers' salaries. Southern workman, 50: 31-34, January 1921.

   Salaries of Negro teachers.

*   Work, Monroe N. See also 165, 290.

456. Wright, Arthur D. Virginia's Negro teachers. Southern workman, 46: 169-72, March 1917.

   Excerpts from the report of the State school inspector in charge of Negro school work in Virginia, for the year ending June 30, 1916. Makes a plea for better teachers.

457. Wright, R.R. The present business possibilities for our race youth. Bulletin (National association of teachers in colored schools), 12: 13-14, 26, 27, December 1931.

   The author states that the business of feeding, clothing, and sheltering the vast Negro group offers opportunities for the Negro with sound education and righteous purpose who, in addition, manifests the capacity for hard work and self-sacrifice.

458. Wright, Richard R., jr. Self-help in Negro education. Cheyney, Pa., Committee of twelve for the advancement of the interests of the Negro race [1909]. 5-29 p. 8°.

Y

459. Yeuell, Gladstone H. The Negro press as a factor
     in education. Journal of educational sociology,
     2: 92-98, October 1928.

460. Yousef, Nagib. The evolution of commercial edu-
     cation in Egypt. International review for
     commercial education, second series, 10: 698-
     701, May 1931.

     An expository account of commercial education
     in Egypt.

Z

461. Zanzibar Protectorate. Annual report of the
     Education department. Zanzibar, The Government
     printer, 1930. 56 p.

Journals Indexed

Adult Bible Class Monthly (Cincinnati) 1, 1908-

Adult Education (Albany, N.Y.) 1-8, 1925-1933
   1-3, 1925-1927 as Interstate Bulletin
   3-7, 1927-1931 as Adult Education Quarterly

Advocate of Peace (Washington, D.C.) 1, 1837-
   title varies

Akademische Rundschau; Zeitschrift für das Gesamte
   Hochschulwesen und die Akademischen Berufstände
   1-8, 1912-1920

Alabama School Journal (Birmingham) 1, 1883-
   1-39, 1883-1921 as Educational Exchange

Alaska School Bulletin (Juneau) 1, 1918-

Albany Medical Annals (Albany, N.Y.) 1, 1880-

Allgemeine Deutsche Lehrerzeitung (Berlin) 1, 1871-
   1-47, 1871-1918 as Paedagogische Zeitung

Allgemeine Deutsche Lehrerzeitung (Leipsiz) 1-66,
   1849-1914

Alrededor de la Escuela; Publicacion Mensual (Havana)
   1-2, 1915-1918

Alumni Bulletin of the Union Theological Seminary

Alumni Bulletin of the University of Virginia

Alumni Register (University of Pennsylvania)

America: A Catholic Review of the Week (New York)
   1, 1909-

American Academy of Political and Social Science. Annals (Phila.) 1, 1890-

American Annals of the Deaf (Washington, D.C.)
   1, 1847-

American Association of University Professors, Bulletin (Easton, Pa.) 1, 1915–

American Association of University Women. Journal (Concord, N.H.) 1, 1884–
to 1920 as the Association of Collegiate Alumnae

American Boy (Detroit) 1–30, 1899–1929; 103, 1930–
Absorbed Youth's Companion and assumed its numbering

American Child: A Journal of Constructive Democracy 1, 1919–

American Childhood 1, 1916–
1916–1926 as Kindergarten and First-Grade Magazine

American City (New York) 1, 1909–

American College (New York) 1–2, 1909–1910

American College Bulletin (Chicago) 1–3, 1928–1929

American Cookery (Boston) 1, 1896–
1–18 as Boston Cooking School Magazine

American Dental Association Journal (Chicago) 1, 1913–

American Education (Albany, N.Y.) 1–32, 1897–1928

American Educational Digest
see School Executive's Magazine

American Educational Review (Chicago) 1–36, 1879–1915

American Federationist (AF of L, Washington, D.C.) 1, 1894–

American Home Economics Association. Bulletin (Baltimore 1, 1912–

American Journal of Care for Cripples (New York) 1–3, 1914–1919

American Journal of Nursing (Rochester, N.Y.) 1, 1900–

American Journal of Physiology (Baltimore) 1, 1898–

American Journal of Public Health and the Nation's Health (Albany, N.Y.) 1, 1911–
1911 as American Public Health Association. Journal 2–17, 1912–1927 as American Journal of Public Health

American Journal of School Hygiene
see School Hygiene Review

American Journal of Sociology (Chicago) 1, 1895–

American Journal of Theology (Chicago) 1-24, 1897–
    1920

American Labor Legislation Review (New York) 1, 1911–

American Law School Review (St. Paul, Minn.) 1, 1902–

American Library Association. Bulletin (Chicago) 1,
    1907–

American Machinist (New York) 1, 1877–

American Magazine (New York) 1, 1876–

American Magazine of Art (New York; Washington, D.C.)
    1, 1909–
    1909-1915 as Art and Progress

American Medical Association. Journal (Chicago) 1,
    1883–

American Motherhood (Cooperstown, N.Y.) 1-49, 1895–
    1919
    see also Mother and Child

American Oxonian (Concord, N.H.) 1, 1914–

American Penman (New York) 1, 1885–

American Physical Education Review 1-34, 1896-1929

American Review (Bloomington, Ind.) 1-4, 1923-1926

American Review of Reviews (New York)
    see Review of Reviews

American School (Milwaukee, Wis.) 1-9, 1915-1923

American School Board Journal (Milwaukee, Wis.)
    1, 1891–

American Schoolmaster (Ypsilanti, Mich.) 1, 1908–

American Shorthand Teacher (New York) 1, 1920–

American Statistical Association. Journal (Boston)
    1, 1888–
    title varies

American Teacher (New York) 1 10, 1912 1921; 1926

Americanization (U.S. Bureau of Education, Washington,
    D.C.) 1, 1918–

Arbitrator (New York) 1, 1918–

Archiv für Pädagogik (Leipzig) 1-4, 1912-1916

Archives of Diagnosis (New York) 1-14, 1908-1922

Arizona Journal of Education (Phoenix) 1-3, 1910-1912

Arizona Teacher (Phoenix) 1, 1914–

Arizona Teacher and Home Journal (Phoenix)

Arkansas School Journal (Little Rock) 1-?, 1896-1913

Arkansas Teacher (Conway) 1-10, 1913-1922

Art and Progress
see American Magazine of Art

Asia (Concord, N.H.; New York) 1, 1898–
1898-1917 as Journal of the American Asiatic Association

Associate Teacher (Pierre, S.D.) 1-18, 1899-1918

Association of American Colleges. Bulletin 1, 1915–

Association of American Medical Colleges. Journal
(Chicago) 1, 1926–
1926-1928 as its Bulletin

Association of Collegiate Alumnae
see American Association of University Women

Association Seminar and Training School Notes (Springfield, Mass.) 1-26, 1891-1918

Athenaeum (London) 1828-1921

Atlantic Educational Journal (Baltimore) 1-13, 1905-1918

Atlantic Monthly (Boston) 1, 1857–

Balance Sheet (Cincinnati) 1, 1919–

Baltimore Bulletin of Education 1, 1923–

Banker-Farmer 1-14, 1913-1927

Barnes Foundation Journal 1-2, 1925-1926

Better Schools (Plainsville, Ohio) 1, 1915-

Biblical World (Chicago) nsv 1-54, 1893-1920

Bibliothèque Universelle et Revue Suisse (Lausanne, Switz.) (ser. 4) 1-115, 1896-1924

Bookman (New York) 1, 1895-

Boston Medical and Surgical Journal
see New England Journal of Medicine

Boston Teachers' News-Letter 1, 1912-

British Journal of Psychology (London) 1, 1904-

British Review (London) 1-12, 1913-1915

Bucknell Alumni Monthly (Lewisburg, Pa.)

Bulletin of High Points in the Teaching of Modern Languages in the High Schools of New York City 1-2, 1917-1918

Bulletin of High Points in the Work of the High Schools of New York City
see High Points in the Work ...

Bulletin of the Pan American Union
see Pan American Union. Bulletin

Business America (New York) nsv 2-16, 1907-1914

Business Educator (Columbus)
see Educator

Business Journal (New York) 1-40, 1877-1916
1877-1910 as Penman's Art

Calcutta Review (Calcutta, India) 1-135, 1844-1912; nsv 1-8, 1913-1920; s3 1, 1921-

California. University. School of Education.
California Vocational News Notes 1-7, 1920-1933
1-6 as its California Vocational Part-Time Newsletter

California Blue Bulletin (Sacramento)

California Quarterly of Secondary Education (Berkeley) 1, 1925-

California Tax Digest
  see Tax Digest

California Taxpayers' Journal 1-4, 1917-1920

Canadian Historical Review (Toronto) 1, 1920-

Canadian Magazine (Toronto) 1, 1893-

Carry On; A Magazine on the Reconstruction of Disabled
  Soldiers and Sailors (U.S. Office of the Surgeon
  General) 1, 1918-

Case and Comment (Rochester, N.Y.) 1, 1894-

Catholic Action 1, 1919-
  title varies

Catholic Educational Review (Washington, D.C.) 1, 1911-

Catholic Historical Review (Washington, D.C.) 1, 1915-

Catholic School Interests (Elmhurst, Ill.) 1, 1922-

Catholic School Journal (Milwaukee) 1, 1901-

Catholic School Work (New York) 1, 1909-

Catholic University Bulletin (Washington, D.C.) 1-34,
  1895-1908; nsv 1, 1932-

Catholic World (New York) 1, 1865-

Century (New York) 1-120, 1870-1930

Character Builder (Los Angeles) 1-45, 1900-1932

Chicago. University. University Record 1-13, 1896-
  1908; nsv 1, 1915-

Chicago Schools Journal 1, 1918-

Child (London) 1, 1910-

Child Health Bulletin (New York) 1, 1925-

Child Labor Bulletin (New York) 1-7, 1912-1919

Child Study (London) 1-13, 1908-1920

Child Study (New York) 1, 1923-
  1 (nos. 1-8) as Federation for Child Study. Bulletin

Child-Welfare Bulletin (Peoria, Ill.) 1-7, 1912-1919

Child-Welfare Magazine (Phila.)
see National Parent-Teacher

Childhood Education (Baltimore) 1, 1924-

Children; the Magazine for Parents (New York)
see Parent's Magazine

China Weekly Review (Shanghai) 1, 1917-
1917-1921 as Millard's Review
1921-1923 as Millard's Weekly Review

Chinese Record (Shanghai)

Chinese Students' Monthly (Baltimore) 1-26, 1905-1930

Christian Advocate (Cincinnati)
see Western Christian Advocate

Christian Education (New York) 1, 1917-
1-2 #10 as American College Bulletin

Christian Education (Washington, D.C.)
see Home and School; a Journal of Christian Education

Christian Education Magazine (Board of Education of
the Methodist Episcopal Church, Nashville) 1,
1911-
1-10 #2 as Christian Education Bulletin
10 #3-12 #2 as Christian Education Monthly

Christian Educator (Washington, D.C.)
see Home and School; a Journal of Christian Education

Christian Student (New York) 1, 1900-

Church School (New York) 1, 1919-

Church School Journal (Cincinnati) 1, 1868-
1900-1925 as Sunday School Journal and Bible Students'
Magazine

Classical Journal (Cedar Rapids, Iowa) 1, 1905-

Classical Weekly (Barnard College, New York)

Cleanliness Journal (New York) 1-6, 1927-1932

Clearinghouse 1, 1920–
  title varies:
    Junior High Clearinghouse
    Junior High School Clearinghouse
    Junior-Senior High School Clearinghouse

Colorado School Journal (Denver) 1, 1885–

Coltura Popolare (Milan, Italy) 1, 1911–

Columbia Alumni News

Columbia Law Review (New York) 1, 1901–

Columbia University Quarterly (New York) 1, 1898–

Commercial Education (Phila.)
  see Journal of Commercial Education

Commercial Teacher (White Water, Wis.) 1, 1916–

Common Ground (West Somerville, Mass.)
  see Massachusetts Teacher

Commonweal (New York) 1, 1924–

Congregationalist (Boston) 1, 1816–
  title varies

Connecticut Schools (Hartford) 1–13, 1920–1932

Constructive Quarterly (New York) 1–10, 1913–1922

Contemporary Review 1, 1866–

Continent (Chicago) 1–57, 1870–1926
  1870–1910 as Interior

Cooperative School Bulletin (Auburn, Ind.) 1–10,
  1922–1931

Cora L. Williams Institute for Creative Education.
  Bulletin (Berkeley, Cal.) 1–23, 1919–1926

Cosmopolitan Student (Hayward, Cal.) 1–78, 1886–1925

Craftsman (New York) 1–31, 1901–1916

Crippled Child (Lorain, Ohio) 1, 1923–

Current Education (Phila.) 1–25, 1896–1921
  1896–1915 as Teacher

Current History (New York) 1, 1914–
    title varies

Curriculum Study and Educational Research Bulletin
    (Board of Education, Pittsburgh)

Delineator (New York) 1, 1873–

Delta Chi Quarterly (Menasha, Wis.)

Dental Cosmos (Phila.) 1, 1859–

Dental Items of Interest (Phila.) 1, 1879–
    1879–1915 as Items of Interest

Detroit Educational Bulletin (Board of Education)

Detroit Journal of Education 1–3, 1920–1923

Deutsche Schule (Leipsiz) 1, 1897–

Dial (Chicago) 1–86, 1880–1929

Domestic Art Review
    see Household Arts Review

École du Travail (Paris) 1–2, 1919–1920

Edinburgh Review (Scotland) 1–250, 1802–1929

Educateur Moderne (Paris) 1–9, 1906–1914

Education (Boston) 1, 1880–

Éducation; Revue des Maîtres (Paris) 1, 1909–
    subtitle varies

Education Bulletin (Trenton, N.J.)

Educational Administration and Supervision (Baltimore)
    1, 1915–

Educational Bi-Monthly (Chicago) 1–11, 1906–1917

Educational Conference (White Water, Wis.)

Educational Digest
    see School Executive's Magazine

Educational Exchange
  see Alabama School Journal

Educational Film Magazine (New York) 1, 1919–

Educational Foundations (New York) 1, 1889–

Educational Issues (Indianapolis) 1, 1920–

Educational Measurement Review (Los Angeles) 1–2,
  1925–1926

Educational Method (New York) 1, 1921–
  1921–1929 as Journal of Educational Method

Educational Monthly
  see Progress ...

Educational News Bulletin (Madison, Wis.) 1–13, 1908–
  1921

Educational Outlook (Phila.) 1, 1926–

Educational Press Bulletin (Springfield, Ill.)

Educational Record (Washington, D.C.) 1, 1920–

Educational Research Bulletin (Board of Education,
  Los Angeles, Cal.)
  see Los Angeles Educational Research Bulletin

Educational Research Bulletin (Ohio State University.
  Bureau of Educational Research, Columbus) 1, 1922–

Educational Review (Fredericton, New Brunswick) 1,
  1887–

Educational Review (New York) 1–76, 1891–1928

Educational Screen and Audio-Visual Guide (Chicago)
  1, 1922–
  title varies

Educational Standards; Official Exponent of the Boston
  Public Schools (Charlestown, Mass.) 1–8, 1916–
  1919

Educational Times (London)

Educator (Columbus, Ohio) 1, 1895–
  8–37, 1931 as Business Educator

Educator-Journal (Indianapolis) 1-24, 1900-1924

Educatore (Arezzo, Italy) 1, 1909-

Elementary English Review (Detroit) 1, 1924-

Elementary School Journal (Chicago) 1, 1900-
2-14, 1901-1914 as Elementary School Teacher

Elementary School Teacher
see Elementary School Journal

Elmira School Bulletin (Elmira, N.Y.)

Empire Review (London) 1, 1901-

Engineering Education (Univ. of Pittsburgh)
see Journal of Engineering Education

English Bulletin (University of Texas, Austin)
see Texas. University, Austin ...

English Journal (Chicago) 1-16, 1912-1927
continued as two editions:
English Journal; College Edition
English Journal; High School Edition

English Leaflet (Boston) 1, 1901-
1901-1914 as New England Association of Teachers of
English. Leaflet

English Review (London) 1, 1908-

Enseignement Public; Revue Pédagogique (Paris) 1,
1878-
1878-1926 as Revue Pédagogique

El Estudiante Latino-Americano (New York) 1, 1918-

Extension Monitor (Eugene, Ore.)

Factory and Industrial Management (New York) 1, 1891-
1891-1916 as Engineering Magazine
1916-1927 as Industrial Management

Federal Council Bulletin (Federal Council of Churches
of Christ in America, New York) 1, 1918-

Federal Employee (Washington, D.C.) 1, 1916-

Fisk University News (Nashville)

Florida Education Association. Journal 1, 1923-

Florida School Exponent (Tallahassee) 1-23, 1894-1916

Florida School Journal (Cocoa, Fla.) 1-29, 1894-1923

Florida Schoolroom
  see Florida School Journal

Food and Health Education
  see Practical Home Economics

Forbes (New York) 1, 1917-

Forecast; America's Pure Food Champion (Phila.) 1, 1910-

Fortnightly Review 1, 1865-

Forum and Century (New York) 1, 1886-
  1886-1930 as Forum

Forward (Southern Sociological Congress, Nashville)
  1-3, 1916-1917

Franklin Institute Journal (Phila.) 1, 1826-

Frauenbildung (Leipzig) 1-22, 1902-1923

Free Poland (New York) 1-6, 1914-1919

Friend (Honolulu, Hawaii) (ser 2) 1, 1852-

Garden and Home Builder 1-47, 1905-1928
  1-39, 1905-1924 as Garden Magazine ...

Geisteskultur (Berlin and Leipzig) 1, 1892-

General Federation Magazine (General Federation of
  Women's Clubs, N.Y.) 1-19, 1903-1920

General Magazine and Historical Chronicle (General
  Alumni Society of the University of Pennsylvania)
  1, 1896-

General Science Quarterly
  see Science Education

Geographic News Bulletin (National Geographic Society
    for the U.S. Bureau of Education) 1, 1919-

Geographical Teacher (London)
    see Geography

Geographischer Anzeiger (Gotha) 1, 1900-

Geography (London) 1, 1901-
    1-13, 1901-1926 as Geographical Teacher

Georgia Education Journal (Georgia Education Assn.,
    Macon) 1, 1908-
    1-15, 1908-1923 as School and Home
    15-18, 1923-1926 as Home, School, and Community

Georgia State School Items (State Dept. of Education,
    Atlanta) 1, 1924-

Gesundheit und Erziehung 1, 1888-
    1-35 as Zeitschrift für Schulgesundheitspflege ...

Golden Belt Teacher (Hays, Kan.) 1, 1916-

Good Housekeeping Magazine (New York) 1, 1885-

Gownsman (Cambridge, England) 1, 1909-

Grade Teacher 1-34, 1892-1926; 43, 1926-
    1-34 as Primary Education

Grande Revue (Paris) 1, 1897-

Granite State Monthly (Concord, N.H.) 1-63, 1877-1930
    1-60 as Granite Monthly
    61-62 as New Hampshire; the Granite State Monthly

Harper's Magazine (New York) 1, 1850-

Harvard Alumni Bulletin (Boston) 1, 1898-

Harvard Graduates' Magazine 1, 1892-

Harvard Law Review 1, 1887-

Harvard Teachers' Association. Leaflet nsv 1-2,
    1915-1916

Harvard Theological Review 1, 1908-

Hawaii Educational Review (Honolulu) 1, 1913-

Hibbert Journal (London and Boston) 1, 1902-

High Points in the Work of the High Schools of New
    York City 1, 1919-
    1-13 #5, 1919-1931 as Bulletin of High Points ...

High School (Oregon University, School of Education,
    Eugene) 1-9, 1923-1932

High School Journal (Chapel Hill, N.C.) 1, 1918-

High School Quarterly (Athens, Ga.) 1, 1912-

High School Teacher (Columbus, Ohio) 1, 1925-

High School Teachers' Association of New York City.
    Bulletin
    1-47, 18??-1914 as its Official Bulletin

High School Teachers' Association of the District of
    Columbia. Bulletin 1, 1909-

Hispanic American Historical Review (Baltimore) 1,
    1918-

Historical Outlook (Phila.) 1, 1909-
    1-9, 1909-1918 as History Teachers' Magazine

History Teachers' Magazine
    see Historical Outlook

Home and School (General Conference of Seventh-Day
    Adventists, Washington, D.C.) 1, 1909-
    1-6 as Christian Education
    7-13 as Christian Educator

Home and School Guest (Stroudsburg, Pa.) 1-11, 1910-
    1920

Home Economics Counselor (Santa Fé, N.M.) 1, 1925-

Home Economist (American Food Journal, Inc., Floral
    Park, N.Y.)
    see Practical Home Economics

Home Progress (Cambridge, Mass.) 1-6, 1912-1917

Home, School, and Community (Atlanta)
    see Georgia Educational Journal

Hospital School Journal (Detroit) 1-18, 1910-1931
   1912-1917 as Van Leuven Browne National Magazine

Household Arts Review (New York) 1-7, 1908-1914
   1908-1909 as Domestic Art Review

Howard University Record (Washington, D.C.) 1-19, 1907-
   1925

Humanistische Gymnasium (Heidelberg) 1, 1890-

Hygeia (Chicago)

Hygiene and Physical Education (Springfield, Mass.)
   1 #1-11, 1909-1910

Idaho Journal of Education (Caldwell; Boise) 1, 1919-
   1-9, 1919-1927 as Idaho Teacher

Idaho Teacher
   see Idaho Journal of Education

Illinois. University. Bulletin (Urbana) 1, 1876-

Illinois Association of Teachers of English Bulletin
   (Urbana) 1, 1909-

Illinois Teacher (Bloomington; Urbana) 1, 1913-

Immigrants in America Review (New York) 1, 1915-

Independent (New York; Boston) 1-121, 1848-1928

Independent Education (New York) 1-3, 1927-1929

Indian Craftsman
   see Red Man

Indian Leader (Haskell Institute, Lawrence, Kan.)
   1, 1897-

Indian School Journal (Chilocco, Okla.) 1, 1900-

Indiana Instructor (Indianapolis) 1, 1916-

Indiana Magazine of History (Indianapolis) 1, 1905-
   1-8, 1905-1913 as Indiana Quarterly Magazine of
   History

Indiana Teacher (Indianapolis) 1 #1-2, 1924; v 69,
    1924-
    supersedes Educator Journal and continues its volume
    numbering with volume 69

Industrial Arts and Vocational Education 1, 1914-
    1-19, 1914-1930 as Industrial Arts Magazine

Industrial Arts Magazine
    see Industrial Arts and Vocational Education

Industrial Economist (Washington, D.C.) 1-4, 1916-
    1918

Industrial Education Magazine (Chicago; Peoria) 1,
    1899-
    1-15, 1899-1914 as Manual Training Magazine
    16-17, 1914-1916 as Manual Training and Vocational
    Education
    18-23, 1916-1922 as Manual Training Magazine

Industrial Management
    see Factory and Industrial Management

Industry (Boston) 1, 1918-

Instructor (New York) 1, 1891-
    title varies

Inter-America (New York) 1-9, 1917-1926

Inter-Mountain Educator (Missoula, Mont.) 1-19,
    1905-1924

International Journal of Ethics (Phila.) 1, 1890-

International Journal of Religious Education (Chicago)
    1, 1924-

International Review of Missions (Edinburgh, Scotland)
    1, 1912-

Internationale Monatsschrift für Wissenschaft, Kunst
    und Technik (Berlin) 1-15, 1907-1921

Internationales Archiv für Schulhygiene (Munich)
    1-9, 1905-1914

Interstate Bulletin: Adult Education (Albany)
    see Adult Education

Iowa Journal of History and Politics (Iowa City) 1, 1903-

Irish Educational Review (Dublin) 1-7, 1907-1914

Iron Age (New York) 1, 1859-

Japan Review (University of Chicago) 1-6, 1916-1922
1-3, 1916-1919 as Japanese Student

Japanese Student
see Japan Review

Jewish Center (New York) 1, 1922-

Johns Hopkins Alumni Magazine (Baltimore)

Journal des Économistes (Paris) (ser. 6) 1, 1904-

Journal of Adult Education (American Association for Adult Education, N.Y.) 1, 1929-

Journal of Adult Education (London) 1, 1926-

Journal of Applied Psychology (Baltimore) 1, 1917-

Journal of Applied Sociology
see Sociology and Social Research

Journal of Arkansas Education (Little Rock) 1, 1923-

Journal of Chemical Education (Easton, Pa.) 1, 1924-

Journal of Commercial Education 1-58, 1885-1929
title varies:
Typewriter and Phonographic World
Phonographic World and Commercial School Review
Typewriter World, Stenographer, and Phonographic World

Journal of Delinquency
see Journal of Juvenile Research

Journal of Education (Academy of the New Church, Bryn Athyn, Pa.) 1, 1901-

Journal of Education (Boston) 1, 1875-

Journal of Education (London) 1, 1867-

Journal of Education and School World (London)
see Journal of Education (London)

Journal of Educational Method
see Educational Method

Journal of Educational Psychology (Baltimore) 1,
1910-

Journal of Educational Research (Bloomington, Ill.)
1, 1920-

Journal of Educational Sociology (New York) 1, 1927-

Journal of Engineering Education (Society for the Promotion of Engineering Education, Lancaster, Pa.)
1, 1910-
1-6 #7, 1910-1916 as the Society's Bulletin
6 #8-14 #12, 1916-1924 as Engineering Education

Journal of Experimental Pedagogy and Training College
Record (London) 1-6, 1911-1922

Journal of Experimental Psychology (Princeton, N.J.)
1, 1916-

Journal of Expression (Boston) 1-6, 1927-1932

Journal of Geography 1, 1902-

Journal of Heredity (American Genetic Assn., Washington, D.C.) 1, 1910-
1-4, 1910-1913 as American Breeders Magazine

Journal of Home Economics (Baltimore) 1, 1909-

Journal of International Relations (Worcester, Mass.)
1-12, 1910-1922
1-9, 1910-1919 as Journal of Race Development

Journal of Juvenile Research (Whittier, Cal.) 1, 1916-
1-12, 1916-1928 as Journal of Delinquency

Journal of Personnel Research
see Personnel Journal

Journal of Physical Education (New York) 1, 1901-
1901-1927 as Physical Training

Journal of Political Economy (Chicago) 1, 1892-

Journal of Psycho-Asthenics (Association of American
Institutions for Feeble-Minded, Faribault, Minn.)
1-22, 1896-1918

Journal of Race Development
    see Journal of International Relations

Journal of Religion (Chicago) 1, 1921-

Journal of Rural Education (National Education Assn.,
    New York) 1-5, 1921-1926

Journal of Social Forces
    see Social Forces

Journal of Social Hygiene (Albany, N.Y.) 1, 1914-
    1-7 as Social Hygiene

Journal of Sociologic Medicine (Easton, Pa.) 1-20,
    1891-1919

Journal of the National Education Association
    see NEA Journal

Journal of the Outdoor Life (New York) 1, 1904-

Journalism Bulletin
    see Journalism Quarterly

Journalism Quarterly (Urbana, Ill.) 1, 1924-
    1-4, 1924-1927 as Journalism Bulletin

Junior High Clearing House
    see Clearinghouse

Junior-Senior High School Clearing House
    see Clearinghouse

Kansas. University. School of Education. Bureau
    of Social Services and Research. Bulletin of
    Education 1, 1926-

Kansas City School Service Bulletin

Kansas Journal of Education (Kansas City)

Kansas School Journal (Topeka; Wichita) 1 #1-11,
    1919-1920

Kansas School Magazine (Emporia) 1-3, 1912-1914

Kansas Teacher
    see Kansas Teacher and Western School Journal

Kansas Teacher and Western School Journal (Topeka) 1,
    1914-
    title varies

Kentucky High School Quarterly (Lexington) 1-13, 1915-
    1927

Kentucky School Journal (Kentucky Education Assn.,
    Louisville) 1, 1920-
    title varies:
    1-3 KEA Bulletin
        KEA Journal

Kindergarten and First-Grade Magazine
    see American Childhood

Kindergarten-Primary Magazine (Manistee, Mich.) 1,
    1888-
    4-19 as Kindergarten Magazine

Kindergarten Review (Springfield, Mass.) 1-26, 1891-
    1915
    1-7 as Kindergarten News

Körperliche Erziehung (Vienna) 1-15, 1905-1919

Labor Clarion (San Francisco) 1, 1902-

Ladies' Home Journal (Phila.) 1, 1883-

Landmark (London) 1, 1919-

Latin Notes (New York) 1, 1923-

Lehrerin (Leipzig) 1, 1884-

Lehrproben und Lehränge aus der Praxis der Höheren
    Lehranstalten (Halle a.d.s., Germany) 1-187,
    1884-1931

Libraries (Chicago) 1-36, 1896-1931
    1896-1925 as Public Libraries

Library Journal (New York) 1, 1876-

Life and Labor (Chicago) 1-11, 1911-1921

Light (National Purity Federation, La Crosse, Wis.)
    6, 1903-

Living Age (Boston) 1, 1844-

London Teacher (London) 1, 1883-

Los Angeles Educational Research Bulletin 1-11, 1921-
1932

Louisiana School Work
see Southern School Work

Louisiana Teachers' Association. Journal (Baton
Rouge) 1, 1923-

McClure's Magazine
see New McClure's Magazine

McEvoy Magazine (Brooklyn, N.Y.) 1-10, 1908-1918
title varies

Magisterio Chihuahuênse (Chihuahua, Mexico) 1, 1910-

Management Review (New York) 1, 1914-
title varies

Manual Arts Bulletin (Minneapolis)

Manual Training and Vocational Education
see Industrial Education Magazine

Manual Training Magazine
see Industrial Education Magazine

Maryland Medical Journal (Baltimore) 1-61, 1877-1918

Massachusetts Teacher (Boston) 1, 1914-
1-10, 1914-1931 as Common Ground

Mathematical Gazette (London) 1, 1894-

Mathematics Teacher (Lancaster, Pa.; New York) 1,
1908-

Medical Record (New York) 1-101, 1866-1922

Medical Times (New York) 1, 1873-

Mental Hygiene (Albany, N.Y.; Concord, N.H.) 1, 1917-

Mercure de France (Paris) 1, 1890-

Methodist Episcopal Church. Board of Education.
Bulletin (South Nashville, Tenn.)

Methodist Review (New York) 1-114, 1818-1931

Michigan Alumnus (Ann Arbor)

Michigan Education Journal (Lansing) 1, 1923-

Middle-West School Review (Omaha) 1, 1908-
1-4 as North Side School Review
5-6 as Nebraska School Review

Midland Review (New York)

Midland Schools (Des Moines) 1, 1885-

Milbank Memorial Fund Quarterly 1, 1923-

Millard's Review of the Far East (Shanghai, China)
see China Weekly Review

Mind and Body (Milwaukee) 1, 1894-

Minerva (Ostende, Belgium) 1, 1891-

Minneapolis Teachers' League. League Strip

Minnesota Alumni Weekly (Minneapolis)

Minnesota Chats (University of Minnesota) 1, 1923-

Minnesota Education Association. Journal
see Minnesota Journal of Education

Minnesota Education Association. Newsletter
(Minneapolis) 1-7, 1914-1920

Minnesota Journal of Education (Minnesota Education
Assn.) 1, 1921-
1-4, 1921-1924 as Minnesota Teacher
5-7, 1924-1927 as the Association's Journal

Minnesota State Normal Schools Quarterly Journal
(Minneapolis) 1, 1915-

Minnesota Teacher
see Minnesota Journal of Education

Missionary Herald (Boston) 1, 1805-

Missionary Review of the World (New York) 1, 1878-

Missions (Boston) 1, 1910-

Mississippi Educational Advance (Jackson) 1, 1911-

Missouri Journal of Education (Kansas City)

Missouri School Journal (Jefferson City) 1, 1883-

Missouri State Teachers' Association. Bulletin
see School and Community

Moderator Topics (Lansing, Mich.) 1-44, 1880-1924

Modern Hospital (St. Louis) 1, 1913-

Modern Language Bulletin
see Modern Language Forum

Modern Language Forum (MLA of Southern California)
1, 1915-
1915-1925 as Modern Language Bulletin

Modern Language Journal (Hunter College, New York)
1, 1916-

Modern Languages (London) 1, 1919-

Modern Medicine
see Nation's Health

Monatschrift für Höhere Schulen (Berlin) 1, 1902-

Monatshefte der Comeniusgesellschaft
see Geisteskultur

Monatshefte für den Naturwissenschaftlichen Unterricht
see Naturwissenschaftliche Monatshefte ...

Monatshefte für Deutsche Sprache und Pädagogik
(Milwaukee) 1, 1899-

Monist (Chicago) 1, 1890-

Montana Education 1, 1924-

Moslem World (London) 1, 1911-

Mother and Child (Baltimore; New York) 1, 1923-
1-3 as American Motherhood

Mother's Homelife (Elgin, Ill.; New York) 1, 1905-
1905-1921 as Mother's Magazine

Mother's Magazine
see Mother's Homelife

Mount Holyoke Monthly (South Hadley, Mass.)

Mountain Life and Work (Berea, Ky.) 1, 1925-

Moving Picture Age (Chicago) 1-5, 1918-1922

Munsey's Magazine (New York) 1-98, 1889-1929

Music (Boston; New York) 1-5 #7, 1925-1930
1-5 #6 as Music and Youth

Music Student (Los Angeles) 1, 1915-

Music Supervisors' Journal (Madison, Wis.) 1, 1914-

Musical America (New York) 1, 1898-

Musical Quarterly (New York), 1, 1915-

N.C.W.C. Bulletin
N.C.W.C. Review
see Catholic Action
N.E.A. Bulletin
see NEA Journal
NEA Journal (Washington, D.C.) 1, 1913-
1913-1920 as N.E.A. Bulletin
1921-   as Journal of the National Education
Association

NEA Research Bulletin (Washington, D.C.) 1, 1923-

Narcotic Education (Washington, D.C.) 1-5, 1927-1931

Nation (New York) 1, 1865-

National Association of Corporation Schools Bulletin
see Management Review

National Association of Teachers in Colored Schools.
Bulletin (Tuskegee Institute) 1, 1922-

National Catholic Educational Association. Bulletin
(Columbus, Ohio) 4, 1908-

National Catholic War Council. Bulletin (Washington,
D.C.)
see Catholic Action

National Catholic Welfare Conference. Bulletin (Washington, D.C.)
see Catholic Action

National Civic Federation Review (New York) 1-5, 1903-1920

National Education (Wellington, N.Z.) 1, 1919-

National Education Association of the U.S. Bulletin
see NEA Journal

National Education Association of the U.S. Journal (Washington, D.C.) 1-3, 1916-1919

National Education Association of the U.S. Department of Elementary School Principals. Bulletin. 1, 1921-

National Efficiency Quarterly (New York) 1, 1918-1919

National Fire Protection Association. Quarterly (Boston) 1, 1907-

National Geographic Magazine (Washington, D.C.) 1, 1888-

National Health (London) 1-22, 1908-1930

National League of Teachers' Associations. Bulletin (Minneapolis) 1-14, 1918-1925; 9-15, 1926-1932

National Municipal Review (Phila.) 1, 1912-

National Notebook Quarterly (Augusta, Ga.), 1-3, 1918-1921

National Parent-Teacher 1, 1906-
1-4 as National Congress of Mothers. Magazine
4-22 as Child-Welfare Magazine
28-34 as Child Welfare

National Republic (Washington, D.C.) 1, 1905-

National Review (London) 1, 1883-

National School Building Journal 1, 1919-

National School Digest
see School Executive's Magazine

National School Service (U.S. Dept. of the Interior, Washington, D.C.) 1, 1918-

National Vocational Guidance Association. Bulletin 1, 1921-
title varies

Nation's Business (Chamber of Commerce of the U.S.) 1, 1912-

Nation's Health (Chicago) 1-9, 1919-1927
1-3 as Modern Medicine

Nation's Schools (Chicago) 1, 1928-

Native American (U.S. Indian Vocational School, Phoenix) 1, 1900-

Nature (London) 1, 1869-

Nature and Science Education Review 1-2, 1928-1930

Nature-Garden Guide 1, 1921-

Nature Magazine (Washington, D.C.) 1, 1923-

Nature Study Review (Ithaca, N.Y.; Chicago) 1-19, 1905-1923

Naturwissenschaftliche Monatshefte für den Biologischen, Chemischen, Geographischen Unterricht (Leipzig) 1-29, 1902-1932

Nebraska Alumnus (Lincoln)

Nebraska Farmer (Lincoln) 1, 1877-

Nebraska School Review
see Middle-West School Review

Nebraska Teacher (Lincoln) 1-25, 1898-1922

Neue Bahnen (Leipzig) 1, 1890-

Nevada Educational Bulletin (Carson City) 1, 1919-

Nevada School Journal (Reno) 1-9, 1909-1918

New England Association of Teachers of English. Leaflet
see English Leaflet

New England Journal of Medicine (Boston) 1, 1828-
1-197, 1828-1928 as Boston Medical and Surgical
Journal

New Era in Home and School (London) 1, 1920-

New Haven Teachers Journal 1, 1907-

New Jersey Journal of Education (Newark) 1-20, 1911-
1931

New Jersey State Research (Newark)

New McClure's Magazine 1-62, 1893-1929
1893-1928 as McClure's Magazine

New Mexico Journal of Education (Santa Fé) 1-17,
1903-1920

New Mexico School Review (N.M. Educational Association)
1, 1921-

New Republic (New York) 1, 1914-

New Student (New York) 1-8, 1922-1929

New York Libraries (Albany) 1, 1907-

New York. Metropolitan Museum of Art. Bulletin
1, 1905-

New York State Education (N.Y. State Teachers'
Association, Albany) 1, 1914-
1-11 #5, 1914-1924 as the Association's Journal

New York State Teachers' Association. Journal
see New York State Education

New York University Alumnus

New Zealand Journal of Education (Dunedin) 1-19,
1899-1917

New Zealand Journal of Science and Technology
(Wellington) 1, 1918-

Newark School Bulletin (Newark, N.J.)

Niagara Index (Niagara University, N.Y.)

Nineteenth Century and After (London) 1, 1877-
title varies

Normal Instructor
see Instructor

Normal School Bulletin (Charleston, Ill.)

North American Review (Boston; New York) 1, 1815-

North Carolina Education (Raleigh) 1-18, 1906-1924

North Carolina High School Bulletin (Chapel Hill)
1-8, 1910-1917

North Carolina Teacher (Raleigh) 1, 1924-

North Central Association. Quarterly 1, 1926-

North Dakota. University. School of Education.
Record 1, 1915-

North Side School Review
see Middle-West School Review

Northwest Journal of Education (Seattle) 1-32, 1889-
1921

Nuova Antologia (Rome) 1, 1866-

Oberlin Alumni Magazine

Ohio Education Association. Department of Elementary
School Principals. Bulletin 1-3, 1927-1930

Ohio Educational Monthly (Columbus) 1-75, 1852-1926

Ohio History Teachers' Journal (Columbus) 1-37,
1916-1925

Ohio Schools (Ohio Educational Association, Columbus)
1, 1923-
1-3 as the Association's Journal

Ohio State University Monthly (Columbus)

Ohio Teacher (Cambridge) 1, 1880-
title varies

Oklahoma Home and School Herald
see Oklahoma School Herald

Oklahoma Journal of Education (Oklahoma City)

Oklahoma School Herald (Oklahoma City) 1-30, 1892-
1922

Oklahoma Teacher (Oklahoma Education Association,
Oklahoma City) 1, 1919-

Old Penn (University of Pennsylvania)

Omaha School Forum

Open Court (Chicago) 1, 1887-

Optimist; A Magazine of the Teacher (Scranton, Pa.)
1, 1904-

Oregon Education Journal (Oregon State Teachers'
Assn., Portland) 1, 1926-

Oregon Law Review (Eugene) 1, 1921-

Oregon State Teachers' Association Quarterly (Salem)
1-8, 1919-1926

Oregon Teacher (Salem) 1-32, 1897-1928

Oregon Teachers' Monthly
see Oregon Teacher

Outlook (New York) 1, 1870-

Outlook and Independent
see Outlook

Pacific Magazine (Seattle) 1-15, 1912-1931

Pädagogische Blätter (Gotha) 1-51, 1872-1922

Pädagogische Studien (Dresden-Blasewitz) nsv 1-48,
1880-1927

Pädagogische Warte (Leipzig) 1, 1893-

Pädagogische Zeitung (Berlin)
see Allgemeine Deutsche ...

Pädagogisches Archiv (Leipzig) 1-56, 1859-1914

Pädagogisches Zentralblatt (Langensalza, Germany)
1, 1919-

Pan-American Union. Bulletin (Washington, D.C.) 1,
1893-

Pan Pacific Progress
see Pacific Magazine

Parents' Magazine (Chicago) 1, 1926–

Parents' Review (London) 1, 1890–

Peabody Journal of Education (Nashville) 1, 1923–

Pedagogical Seminary (Worcester, Mass.) 1, 1891–

Pennsylvania Gazette (University of Pennsylvania)

Pennsylvania Medical Journal (Athens) 1, 1897–

Pennsylvania School Journal (Lancaster) 1, 1852–

Pentathlon 1-2, 1928-1929

Personnel
see Management Review

Personnel Journal (Baltimore) 1, 1922–
1922-1927 as Journal of Personnel Research

Philippine Education
see Philippine Magazine

Philippine Magazine (Manila) 1, 1904–

Philippine Review (Manila) 1-6, 1916-1921

Philosophical Review (Boston; etc.) 1, 1892–

Physical Culture (New York) 1, 1899–

Physical Training
see Journal of Physical Education

Pictorial Review (New York) 1, 1899–

Pittsburgh. University. School of Education.
Journal 1-6, 1925-1931

Pittsburgh School Bulletin 1, 1907–

Platoon School (National Association for the Study of
the Platoon, or Work-Study-Play School Organization)
1, 1927–

Playground
see Recreation

Political Quarterly (London) 1, 1930-

Popular Educator (Boston) 1-43, 1885-1926

Popular Science Monthly (New York) 1, 1872-

Porto Rico School Review (San Juan) 1, 1917-

Posse Gymnasium Journal (Boston) 1-28, 1892-1920

Practical Home Economics 5, 1927-
Ja-S 1927 as Food and Health Education
Oc 1927-F 1928 as Home Economist
Mr-D 1928 as Home Economist and the American Food
Journal

Practical School Journal (Litchfield, Ill.) 1-8,
1911-1918

Praxis der Arbeitsschule München 1, 1910-

Preussische Jahrbücher (Berlin) 1, 1858-

Primary Education
see Grade Teacher

Primary Plans
see Instructor

Princeton Alumni Weekly

Printing Education (Chicago) 1, 1923-

Printing Instructor
see Printing Education

Progress: A Magazine for the New Day (Chicago) 1-11,
1917-1927
1917-1925 as Social Progress

Progress; A National Journal of Education, Industry,
and Social Service (Athens, Ga.)
1-2 #6, 1915-1916
1-2 #1 as Educational Monthly

Progressive Education (Washington, D.C.) 1, 1924-

Progressive Teacher (Nashville) 1, 1895-
title varies

Providence Public School Bulletin

Psychoanalytic Review (Lancaster, Pa.) 1, 1913–

Psychological Bulletin (Princeton, N.J.) 1, 1904–

Psychological Clinic (Phila.) 1, 1907–

Psychological Review (Lancaster, Pa.; Princeton, N.J.)
  1, 1894–

Public (New York) 1–22, 1898–1919

Public Health Nurse 1, 1909–
  title varies

Public Libraries
  see Libraries

Public School Bulletin (Atlantic City, N.J.)

Public School Messenger (St. Louis) 1, 1899–

Public Servant (Madison, Wis.) 1–2, 1916–1917

Publishers Weekly (New York) 1, 1872–

Quarterly Journal of Public Speaking
  see Quarterly Journal of Speech

Quarterly Journal of Speech (Chicago) 1, 1915–
  1915–1917 as Quarterly Journal of Public Speaking
  1918–1927 as Quarterly Journal of Speech Education

Quarterly Journal of Speech Education
  see Quarterly Journal of Speech

Quarterly Journal of the University of North Dakota

Quarterly Review (London) 1, 1809–

Queen's Quarterly (Kingston, Canada) 1, 1893–

Recalled to Life; A Journal Devoted to the Care, Re-
  education, and Return to Civil Life of Disabled
  Sailors and Soldiers (London) 1, 1917–

Reclamation Era (U.S. Bureau of Reclamation, Washington, D.C.) 1, 1908–
  1908 as its Monthly Bulletin
  1908–1924 as Reclamation Record
  1924–1931 as New Reclamation Era

Recreation 1, 1907–
1907-1929 as Playground

Red Cross Magazine (New York) 1-15, 1906-1920
title varies

Red Man (Carlisle, Pa., Indian Industrial School)
1-9, 1909-1917
1-2 #5, 1909-1910 as Indian Craftsman

Relief Society Magazine (Salt Lake City) 1, 1914–

Religious Education (Chicago) 1, 1906–

Review of Reviews (New York) 2, 1890–

Revista de Instruccion Pública (Havana, Cuba) 1-3;
(s2) 1-4; 1918-1928

Revista de la Facultad de Letras Ciencias (University
of Havana, Cuba)

Revue de l'Enseignement des Langues Vivantes (Paris)
1, 1884–

Revue de Paris 1, 1894–

Revue des Deux Mondes (Paris) 1, 1831–

Revue Internationale de l'Enseignement (Paris) 1,
1881–

Revue Pédagogique
see Enseignement Public

Revue Politique et Parlementaire (Paris) 1, 1894–

Revue Universitaire (Paris) 1, 1892–

Rivista Pedagogica (Rome) 1, 1908–

Round Table (London) 1, 1910–

Rural Education (Aberdeen, S.D.) 1, 1919–

Rural Educator (Columbus, Ohio) 1-7, 1913-1916

Rural Manhood (New York) 1-11, 1910-1920

Rural School Messenger (Kirksville, Mo.) 1-13, 1912-
1923

Rural School Teacher (Chicago) 1, 1915–

Safeguarding America against Fire (New York) 1, 1917–

Safety Education (New York) 1, 1924–
1924-1925 as Bulletin of Safety Education

Saturday Evening Post (Phila.) 1, 1821–

Scholastic (Pittsburgh) 1, 1920–
title varies

Scholastic Editor (Madison, Wis.) 3, 1923–
1-2 mimeo

School; Devoted to the Public Schools and Educational
Interests (New York) 1, 1889–

School; A Magazine Devoted to Elementary and Secondary
Education (Toronto) 1, 1912–

School and Community (Buffalo, N.Y.) 1 #1-21, 1919–
1920

School and Community (Missouri State Teachers' Assn.,
Columbia) 1, 1915–
1-6 as its Bulletin

School and Home (Atlanta)
see Georgia Education Journal

School and Home (Ethical Culture School, New York)
1, 1918–

School and Home Education (Bloomington, Ill.) 1-41,
1881-1922

School and Science Review (Austin, Tex.)

School and Society 1, 1915–

School Arts (Boston) 1, 1901–
title varies

School Bulletin and New York State Education (Syracuse) 1-47, 1874-1920

School Education
see School Executive's Magazine

School Executive's Magazine (Minneapolis?) 1, 1881-
1883-1920 as School Education
1920-1922 as National School Digest
1922 as Educational Digest
1923-1928 as American Educational Digest

School Guardian (London) 1, 1876-

School Hygiene (London) 1-12, 1910-1921

School Hygiene Review (Worcester, Mass.) 1-7, 1917-
1923
1-5 as American Journal of School Hygiene

School Index (Cincinnati)

School Journal (New York) 1-81, ns 1; 1871-1916

School Life (U.S. Bureau of Education, Washington,
D.C.) 1, 1918-

School Music (Keokuk, Iowa) 1, 1900-

School Music Review (London) 1-38, 1892-1930

School News (Syracuse, N.Y.) 1-2, 1925-1927

School News and Practical Educator (Chicago; etc.)
1, 1887-

School News of New Jersey
see New Jersey Journal of Education

School Progress for Teachers, Parents, and Pupils
(Phila.) 1-7, 1909-1916

School Review (Chicago) 1, 1893-

School Science and Mathematics (Chicago) 1, 1901-

School Teacher (Washington, D.C.) 1-3, 1909-1910

School Topics (Cleveland Board of Education) 1-14,
1917-1932

School World (London) 1-20, 1899-1918

Schooling (Sydney, N.S.W.) 1, 1917-

Schoolmaster and Woman Teacher's Chronicle (London)
1, 1872-

Schools and People (Chicago)

Schulhaus (Berlin) 1-24, 1891-1929

Schweizerische Lehrerzeitung (Zurich) 1, 1855-

Science 1, 1883-

Science Education (Salem, Mass.; etc.) 1, 1916-
    1-13, 1916-1929 as General Science Quarterly

Science News Letter (Baltimore) 1, 1921-
    title varies

Scientific American 1, 1845-

Scientific Monthly (Washington, D.C.) 1, 1915-

Scientific Temperance Journal (Boston; Westerville,
    Ohio) 1, 1892-

Scottish Educational Journal (Edinburgh) 1, 1918-

Scouting (New York) 1, 1913-

Scribner's Magazine (New York) 1, 1887-

Seattle Grade Club Magazine 1, 1920-

Sewanee Review (Sewanee, Tenn.) 1, 1892-

Sierra Educational News (San Francisco) 1, 1905-

Silent Worker (Trenton, N.J.) 1-41, 1888-1929

Simmons College Review (Boston)

Smith Alumnae Quarterly

Social Forces (Chapel Hill, N.C.) 1, 1922-
    1-3 as Journal of Social Forces

Social Hygiene
    see Journal of Social Hygiene

Social Progress
    see Progress; A Magazine ...

Social Science (Pi Gamma Mu, Winfield, Kan.) 1,
    1925-

Social Service Review (Washington, D.C.) 1-10, 1915-
    1920

Society for the Promotion of Engineering Education.
   Bulletin
   see Journal of Engineering Education

Sociology and Social Research 6, 1921–
   6–11, 1921–1927 as Journal of Applied Sociology

South Atlantic Quarterly (Durham, N.C.) 1, 1902–

South Carolina Education (University of South Carolina,
   Columbia) 1, 1919–

South Dakota Education Association. Journal (Sioux
   Falls) 1, 1925–

South Dakota Educator (Mitchell) 1–38, 1888–1925

Southern School Journal (Louisville, Ky.) 1–38, 1889–
   1927

Southern School News (Columbia, S.C.) 1–?, 1909–1919

Southern School Work (Alexandria, La.) 1–10, 1913–
   1922
   1–6 as Louisiana Schoolwork

Southern Textile Bulletin (Charlotte, N.C.) 1, 1911–

Southern Workman (Hampton, Va.) 1, 1872–

Southwestern School Review (Austin, Tex.)

Special Libraries (New York) 1, 1910–

Spelman Messenger (Spelman College, Atlanta, Ga.)
   1, 1885–

Standard (American Ethical Union, New York) 1, 1914–

Stanford Alumnus

Stanford Illustrated Review

State Service (Albany, N.Y.) 1, 1917–

Storyteller's Magazine (New York) 1–6, 1913–1918

Sunday School Journal
   see Church School Journal

Survey (New York) 1–68, 1897–1932

Tax Digest (Los Angeles) 1, 1925–
  1925–1926 as California Tax Digest

Teacher
  see Current Education

Teachers College Record (Teachers College, Columbia
  University) 1, 1900–
  title varies

Teachers' Journal (Marion, Ind.) 1–19, 1901–1920

Teachers' Journal (New Haven, Conn.)
  see New Haven Teachers Journal

Teachers Journal and Abstract (Colorado State
  Teachers College, Greeley) 1–7, 1926–1932

Teachers' Monographs (New York) 1–35, 1897–1928

Teachers World (London) 1, 1913–

Teaching (Kansas State Teachers' College, Emporia)
  1–11, 1914–1932

Techne (Kansas State Teachers College, Pittsburg)
  1, 1915–

Technology Review (Massachusetts Institute of Technology, Cambridge) 1, 1899–

Tennessee School Record (Alexandria) 1, 1917–

Texas Outlook (Texas State Teachers Association,
  Fort Worth) 1, 1916–
  1–3, 1916–1919 as its Bulletin

Texas School Board Journal (Dallas) 1; nsv 1–47,
  1882–1932

Texas School Magazine (Dallas) 1–17, 1898–1914

Texas State Teachers Assn. Bulletin
  see Texas Outlook

Texas. University, Austin. English Bulletin
  1, 1911–

Theatre and School (Berkeley, Cal.) 1, 1922–

Times (London) Educational Supplement 1, 1910–

Trained Men (International Correspondence School,
    Scranton, Pa.) 1, 1921-

Trained Nurse and Hospital Review (New York) 1, 1888-

Training School Bulletin (Vineland, N.J.) 1, 1904-
    title varies

Training School Quarterly (Greenville, N.C.)

Trans-Pacific (Tokyo) 1, 1919-

Tsing Hua Journal (Tsing Hua College, Peking) 1,
    1924-

Tuskegee Student (Tuskegee Institute) 1-34, 1884-
    1924

Ungraded (New York; Albany) 1-11, 1915-1926

University High School Journal (Oakland, Cal.) 1,
    1921-

University Journal (Lincoln, Neb.)

University of California Chronicle (Berkeley)

Unpartizan Review (New York) 1-15, 1914-1921
    1-11 as Unpopular Review

Unpopular Review
    see Unpartizan Review

Utah Educational Review (Salt Lake City) 1, 1907-

Van Leuven Browne National Magazine
    see Hospital School Journal

Vanderbilt University Quarterly (Nashville) 1-15,
    1901-1915

Vassar Journal of Undergraduate Studies (Poughkeepsie,
    N.Y.) 1, 1926-

Virginia Journal of Education (Richmond) 1, 1907-

Virginia State Teachers' Association. Quarterly
    (Richmond) 1-4, 1915-1918

Virginia Teacher (Harrisonburg) 1, 1920–

Vision (Bureau of Commercial Economics, Washington, D.C.)

Visitor; Devoted to the Interests of Agriculture and Manual Training in Minnesota High Schools (University of Minnesota Farm, St. Paul) 1, 1914–

Visual Education 1–5, 1920–1924

Vocational Education (Peoria) 1–3, 1911–1914

Vocational Education News Notes
    see California. University. School of Education ...

Vocational Guidance Magazine 1, 1921–
    title varies

Vocational Summary (Federal Board for Vocational Education, Washington, D.C.) 1, 1918–

Vocationist (Oswego, N.Y.) 1, 1912–

Volta Review (Washington, D.C.) 1, 1899–

Vor Ungdom (Copenhagen) 1879–1928

Washington Academy of Sciences. Journal 1, 1911–

Washington Education (Seattle) 1, 1921–
    title varies

Weekly Review (New York) 1–5, 1919–1921

West Virginia Educator (Charleston) 1–9, 1907–1915

West Virginia School Journal (Wheeling) 1, 1881–

West Virginia School Journal and Educator (Charleston) 1, 1881–

Western Christian Advocate (Cincinnati) 1–95, 1834–1929
    1929 as Christian Advocate; Western Edition

Western Education (Salem, Ore.) 1928–1929

Western Journal of Education (San Francisco) 1, 1895–

Western School Journal (Topeka) 1–32, 1885–1916

Western Teacher (Milwaukee) 1-28, 1892-1920

Westminster Review (London) 1-181, 1824-1924

Westonian (Westtown, Pa.) 1, 1895-

Wilson Library Bulletin (New York) 1, 1914-
1-13 as Wilson Bulletin

Winona Normal Bulletin (Winona, Mich.)

Wisconsin Educational Horizon (Madison) 1, 1919-

Wisconsin Journal of Education (Madison) nsv 1, 1871-

Woman Citizen
see Woman's Journal

Woman's Journal 1-16, 1917-1931
1-12 as Woman Citizen

Woman's Press 1, 1907-
1907-1922 as YWCA Magazine

Workers Education (New York) 1, 1923-

World Today (London) 1-60, 1902-1932
1902-1923 as World's Work

World's Work (Garden City, N.Y.) 1-61, 1900-1932

World's Work (London)
see World Today

Wyoming Educational Bulletin (Cheyenne) 1, 1919-

Wyoming School Journal (Laramie) nsv 1-15, 1903-1919

YWCA Magazine
see Woman's Press

Yale Alumni Review (New Haven)

Yale Alumni Weekly

Yale Review (New Haven) 1-19, 1892-1911; nsv 1, 1911-

Zeitschrift für Geschichte der Erziehung und des
Unterrichts (Berlin) 1, 1911-

Zeitschrift für Kinderforschung (Langensalza, Germany;
    Berlin) 1, 1896-

Zeitschrift für Lateinlose Höhere Schulen (Leipzig)
    1-30, 1889-1919

Zeitschrift für Padagogische Psychologie (Leipzig)
    1, 1899-
    title varies

Zeitschrift für Philosophie und Padagogik (Langensalza,
    Germany) 1-21, 1894-1914

Zeitschrift für Schulgesundheitspflege (Leipzig)
    see Gesundheit ...

Zuid en Noord (Ghent) 1-3, 1910-1912

Index

Accreditation 43, 108, 294, 392
Achievements 309
Activities 320, 440
Administration 45, 52, 67, 265, 343
Adult education 68, 246
Africa 7, 19, 48, 49, 55A, 58, 59, 62, 100, 116, 121,
148, 157, 158, 159, 177, 180, 185, 186, 213, 219,
225, 237, 254, 258, 275, 300, 303, 304, 315, 357,
358, 377, 378, 390, 391, 396, 397, 398, 400, 401,
402, 406, 407, 427, 434, 436, 452, 460, 461
African children 100, 225, 406, 427, 434
African culture 186
African Education Commission 7
Agricultural education 38, 54, 70, 77, 109, 126, 165,
252, 308, 411, 418
Al Azhar University, Cairo, Egypt 13
Alabama 246, 356
  Birmingham 45
  Calhoun 447
  Madison County 252
  Russell County 333
  Tuskegee 41
Alabama Polytechnic Institute 252
American Education Week 46, 404
American history textbooks 51
American University, Beirut 185
American University, Cairo 185
Americanization 228, 270
Animal-like behavior 194
Anna T. Jeanes Foundation 16, 95, 102, 103, 108,
110, 123, 125, 146, 250, 298, 334, 445
Anthropology 396
Applied knowledge 12
Arabic language 254
Arithmetic 233

Armstrong, Samuel C.   229, 448
Art   10, 33
Asia   55A
Association of County Superintendents   451
Association tests   268
Atlanta University   192, 292
Attendance   43, 66, 76, 130, 207, 294, 432
Attitudes   113, 142

Bahamas   61
Baptist Church   40
Barbados   17
Basutoland   19
Belgian Congo   427
Belgium   427
Berea College   20
Bermuda   21
Bibliography   22, 42, 46, 80, 124, 242, 302, 311, 318,
    374, 375, 450, 452
Biddle College   265
Binet tests   272, 317, 375, 381
Birmingham, Ala., Industrial High School   45
Blacksmithing   163
Board of Education, Methodist Episcopal Church   187
Booker T. Washington High School, Enid, Okla.   227
Booker T. Washington School, Dover, Del.   174
Bordentown School   32
Border States   313
Boston University   318
Bovard, William S.   261
Boys   39, 118, 435
Bricklaying   163
British Guiana   34
British Honduras   107
Broadneck Farm, Hanover Co., Va.   118
Brooks, E.C.   101
Buildings   66, 108, 122, 205, 280, 292, 298
Bureau of Education. *See* U.S. Bureau of Education
Business   457
Businessmen   192

Cabinetmaking 162, 163
Calabar Mission 436
Calhoun School, Ala. 447
Caliver, Ambrose 150
Canada 161
Canal Zone 114
Cape of Good Hope 48
Carnegie Corporation of New York 125, 260
Carnegie Foundation for the Advancement of Teaching
    16, 125
Carnegie Institution of Washington 16
Carpentry 162, 163
Catawba College 52, 232
Catholic education 53, 243, 270, 271, 355
Catholic Educational Association 53
Census 215, 423
Centralization of schools 48
Certification 245
Character 395
Cheyney Training School for Teachers 183
Child study 123, 341
Child welfare work 406
Children, African 100, 225, 406, 427, 434
Children's court 210
Christian education 55A, 159
Christianity 63, 111
Churches 31
Cities 313, 368
Civic project 440
Civics 233
Civil War 450
Clark, Ismael 322
Clark College 265
Clark Co. Training School, Athens, Ga. 337
Classical education /3
Classrooms 294
Claxton, P.P. 65
Clayton, R.A. 368
College centers 124
Colleges 115, 123
Colonial University of Belgium 427
Columbia University 237, 242, 302, 374

Columbus Memorial Library, Washington, D.C.   399
Commerce   39, 238
Commercial education   460
Commission on Interracial Cooperation   108
Commissioner of Education   328, 329, 408, 409
Committee of Twelve for the Advancement of the In-
    terests of the Negro Race   74, 458
Commonwealth Fund   125
Community   27, 165, 191
Community centers   174
Compulsory education   107
Conference for Education in the South   64, 65, 74
Conference on Dual Education   260
Congo   427
Consolidations   190
Consonance   374
Cost of instruction   66
Council of Women for Home Missions   161
County training schools   91, 92, 93, 134, 356
Crime   371
Crippled children   307
Cuba   37, 181, 262, 269, 291, 322, 331, 341, 355,
    399, 403, 408
Cultural experiences   335
Curriculum, college   52
Cuyler Street School, Savannah, Ga.   14

Danish folk schools   139
Declaration of Geneva   100
Delaware   76
    Dover   174
Delinquents   210
Demography   336, 427
Denmark   139, 420
    Askov   139
Department of State   410
Department of Superintendence   104, 266, 279, 280
Distribution of schools   43, 132
District of Columbia   39, 343, 399
Domestic art   233
Domestic servants   77

Douglass High School, Cincinnati, Ohio   230
Drake, Amy B.   415
Dramatic art   233
Drawing   233
Drums   58
Dual system.   *See* Separate school systems
Duplication of schools   442

Economic efficiency   301
Economic history   430
Economic progress/status   33, 417
Educational reconstruction   140
Efficiency   437
Egypt   75, 85, 460
  Cairo   13, 185, 397
Elementary schools   411
Emancipation   175
Employment   54, 77
England, London   84
English Americans   51
English language   29, 233, 434
English people   51
Enrollment   43, 190, 207, 244, 432
Equatorial Africa   7
Equipment, teaching   245, 431, 432
Evening school   411
Expenditure.   *See* Finance
Extracurricular activities   233

Faculties, college   190
Farmers   326
Fayetteville, N.C., State Normal School   350
Feagin, William F.   366, 377
Federal Board for Vocational Education   325, 411
Federal service in the education of Negroes   43
Feebleminded children   60
Fellowships   123
Finance   47, 244, 285, 290
First Universal Races Congress   409
Fisher, Isaac   347

Fisk University   212, 273
Florida, Daytona   344
Florida Agricultural and Mechanical College   220
Folk games   11
Foreign language   434
Foreign missions   7
Foreign-born   228
Fort Valley, Ga., Industrial School   138
Frederick Douglass Junior High School, New York City
   395
Free Education   48
Freshman Week   154
Freshmen, college   119, 154, 379
Frissell, Hollis Burke   82, 188, 303A

The Gambia   62
Games   11
Gardens   233
Garland Fund   286
Garrison Demonstration School, Washington, D.C.   343
Gates, G.S.   217
General education   54, 123, 216
General Education Board   16, 82, 93, 97, 108, 123,
   125, 145, 146
Geography   180, 233, 417
George Peabody College   260
Georgia   39, 54, 108, 120, 285
   Athens   337
   Atlanta   156
   Augusta   190A
   Clarke Co.   184
   Peach Co.   138
   Savannah   14, 451
German-Americans   51
Gifted children   60
Girls   239, 240, 417, 435
Girls' schools   177
Goddard, H.H.   272
Gold Coast   148
Grading   182
Graduate work   245

Granada   155
Grants   123
Grouping   182
Guerra, Ramiro   399

Haiti   243, 410
Hampton Institute   2, 5, 6, 70, 87, 94, 97, 109, 162,
    163, 167, 168, 169, 170, 171, 188, 211, 229, 239,
    303A, 311, 324, 326, 388, 389, 441, 444, 448
Hampton Negro Conference   164, 165, 166
Handicapped children   307
Happiness   420
Harlem   395
Harriet Beecher Stowe School, Cincinnati, Ohio   305
Harris, T.H.   128
Hawaii   408
Health   123, 151, 216, 218, 299, 301, 335, 395
Health education   9, 233, 249, 299
Height   276
High schools   39, 43, 294, 298
Higher education   10, 43, 44, 80, 105, 112, 115, 117,
    146, 154, 190, 216, 221, 232, 236, 238, 255, 259,
    265, 266, 287, 290, 294, 298, 330, 331, 366, 394,
    397, 400, 425, 453, 454
History   51, 233, 431
Home economics   199, 240, 324, 331
Homemaking   241
Homes, teachers'   108
Hospitals   307
House, S. Daniel   379
Howard, F.W.   53
Howard University   117, 273, 379
Hunley, W.M.   414

Ideals   309
Illinois intelligence scale   127
Illiteracy   10, 75, 205, 228, 246, 257, 322, 423
Income and expenditures   43
Individual needs   27
Industrial education   10, 14, 30, 31, 45, 70, 71, 73,
    83, 91, 92, 146, 159, 162, 190A, 251, 335, 371, 436

Industrial teachers 91
Inglis, Alexander J. 416
Inherited traits 143
Instituto de segunda ensenanza, Matauzas, Cuba 403
Intellectuals 157
Intelligence quotient 119, 136
Intelligence scores 144, 344, 349
Intelligence studies 15, 222, 226, 309, 316, 433
International Conference on the African Child 225
Interracial relationships 198
Irish-Americans 51
Ironsides School, Bordentown, N.J. 32, 152
Italian-Americans 51

Jamaica 200, 201
Jazz 338
Jeanes Fund. *See* Anna T. Jeanes Foundation
Jebb, Eglantyne 100, 225
Jews 424
John F. Slater Fund for the Education of Freedmen
    16, 30, 93, 95, 108, 123, 125, 134, 146, 202,
    203, 204, 234, 442, 445
Joint Committee on Negro Child Study in New York City
    210
Jones, Thomas Jesse 126, 179, 190, 287
Joubert, M. 355
Julius Rosenwald Fund 108, 122, 123, 125, 216, 333,
    337, 345, 424
Junior colleges 146
Junior high schools 395

Kansas
  Kansas City 349
  Leavenworth 355
Kentucky 15, 20, 124
  Louisville 238
Kenya 219
  Kabete 110
  Mombasa 406
Kindergarten 331

Kingdom of Tonga 398
Klein, Arthur J. 384
Knoll papers 2

Labor 430
Land-grant colleges 38, 221
Language 182, 434
Laws 285, 294, 342
Leadership 267
League of Nations 100, 225
Leeward Islands 231
Leisure time 346
Liberia 121
Libraries 66, 108, 123, 190, 290, 331, 335, 349, 399
Literacy 10, 69. *See also* Illiteracy
Literature 10, 33, 116
Locomotion 194
London, England 84
Louisiana 128, 133, 242, 426
  New Orleans 114, 381
Lynching 413

McCleery, Ada Belle 284

Machine work 163
Mann, Gertrude C. 203, 204
Manual training 233
Manual Training and Industrial School for Colored
    Youth, Bordentown, N.J. 32
Marie, A. 336
Maryland 195
  Baltimore 355
  Ridge 355
Mauritius 258
Measurements. *See* Tests and measurements
Mechanical departments 393
Medical education 146, 176
Medical inspection 48
Mental ability 86, 137, 205, 272

Mental growth 144, 446
Mental health 379
Methodist Church 187, 261, 373
Methods of teaching 411, 431
Middle class 71
Migration 178, 205, 413
Ministers 298, 326
Missionary education movement 161
Missions 7, 33, 59, 124, 159, 161, 372, 396, 436
Mississippi 286, 302, 364
  Coahoma Co. 129
Missouri 38, 342
  St. Louis 355
Mohammedanism 13
Monroe general-survey test 127
Monroe standardized silent-reading test 127
Montori, Arturo 322
Moral development 175, 388, 440, 446
Morale 380
Morality 301
Morehouse College 265
Morocco 157
Morrill Act 221
Motion pictures 338
Movable schools 252
Music 4, 58, 208, 233, 338, 374
Music School Settlement for Colored People 4

Narcotic education 262
Nash, Nina M. 365
Natal 237
National Association for the Advancement of Colored
    People 133
National Association of Teachers in Colored Schools
    38, 77, 99, 131, 190, 220, 227, 277, 299, 343,
    344, 360, 404, 440, 454
National Education Association 79, 278, 279, 280,
    281, 282, 283
National League of Nursing Education 284
National Negro Conference 306
National Survey of School Finance 47, 150

National Survey of Secondary Education   47, 150
National Survey of the Education of Teachers   47, 150
National Urban League   210
Native culture   197
Nature   135, 233
Neal, H.J.   293
Neglected children   210
Negro Organization Society, Norfolk, Va.   96
Negro Organization Society of Virginia   439
Negro Teachers' Association and School Improvement
    League of Virginia   289, 383
Negro Yearbook   453
New Jersey   293
  Bordentown   32, 152
New Jersey State Teachers' Association   293
New York
  Buffalo   40
  New York   4, 23, 210, 247, 268, 374, 395
Nigeria   300
Night schools   411
Non-verbal tests   382
Normal children   60
Normal College for Men and Women Students, Pretoria,
    South Africa   401
Normal School of Habana, Cuba   399
Normal schools   146, 399, 401
North   178, 205, 263, 303, 432
North Carolina   8, 39, 65, 67, 191, 286, 288, 294,
    295, 296, 297, 298, 307, 360, 392
  Fayetteville   350
  Henderson   207
  Newton   232
  Salisbury   52, 232
Northern Baptist Convention   40
Northern Rhodesia   303
Nuns   355
Nurses' training   146, 284
Nurture   143

Objectives   440
Oblate Sisters of Providence   355

Occupational choice 39, 238
Ohio, Cincinnati 230, 305
Oklahoma
  Enid 227
  Muskogee 114
  Oklahoma City 226
One-room schools 66
Organization of school systems 48
Over-age students 57
Oxford University 236

Painting 163
Pan American Union 399
Parents 294
Part-time school 411
Paul L. Dunbar School, Norfolk, Va. 57
Peabody Education Fund 16
Penmanship 233
Penn School, South Carolina 69, 70, 82, 87, 89
Pennsylvania
  Philadelphia 10, 27, 142
  South Philadelphia 417
Phelps Stokes Fellowship Studies 184, 309
Phelps Stokes Fund 7, 123, 125, 214, 287, 363
Phenix, George P. 97
Phenix School 97
Philosophy of education 52, 67
Physical education 331, 439
Physical plant 45
Pi Lambda Theta 318
Plastering 163
Plumbing 163
Polish-Americans 51
Poll taxes 31
Popular education 269
Population 66, 178
Porters 160
Porto Rico 408
Prejudice 198, 318
President of the U.S. 410
Press 459

Primary instruction 403
Principals 335, 432, 447
Private education 287, 331
Problems of democracy 142, 417
Professional education 71, 73, 331
Professions 39, 238, 435
Progress 419, 428
Property taxes 31
Prosperity 420
Psychogalvanic reactions 60
Psychology 137, 143, 197, 317, 396
Public education 43, 50, 112, 124, 141, 149, 190A,
    216, 244, 288A, 356, 361, 362, 416
Public Education Association of the City of New York
    23
Public health reports 151
Public health service 299
Puerto Rico. *See* Porto Rico
Pullman porters 160

Race 51, 86, 143
Race relations 56, 198, 206, 260
Racial attitudes 142
Racial good-will 94
Radio 338
Ratio, pupil-teacher 245
Reading 233, 349, 434
Reconstruction 223, 224, 417
Recreation 352, 439
Reformatories 118
Religion 31, 175, 372
Research and publication 43
Rhodesia 158, 303
Rhythm 209, 374
Robert College, Constantinople 185
Rockefeller Foundation 125
Rose, Wickliffe 64
Rosenwald, Julius 424
Rosenwald Fund. *See* Julius Rosenwald Fund
Ruckmick Series 217
Ruggedness 153

Rural industries   135
Rural life   91, 92, 135, 184, 278, 435
Rural schools   66, 69, 70, 98, 106, 135, 205, 278,
    283, 364, 366, 368
Russell Sage Foundation   16

S.A.T.C.   170
St. Lucia   339
St. Vincent   340
Salaries   43, 190, 205, 245, 335, 432, 455
Save-the-Children Fund   100
Schofield, Martha   256
Schofield School, Aiken, S.C.   256
Scholarships   298
School of Arts and Trades, Habana, Cuba   331
Science   347
Scotch-Irish Americans   51
Seashore, Carl E.   208, 209
Seashore music talent tests   208, 209
Secondary schools   29, 44, 47, 108, 113, 141, 230,
    259, 330, 331, 335, 371, 392, 417, 431, 435, 453,
    454
Secretary of the Interior   228
Segregated schools.   See Separate school systems
Segregation   267
Self-expression   234
Self-help   33
Seniors, high school   435
Separate school systems   43, 50, 245, 260, 342
Seychelles   353, 354
Shepherd, Irwin   282
Sierra Leone   177, 357, 358
6 - 3 - 3   182
Slater Fund.   See John F. Slater Fund for the Educa-
    tion of Freedmen
Slavery   124, 450
Sociability   301
Social behavior   304
Social conditions   417
Social hygiene   336
Social perception   217

Social progress 33
Social science 207
Social Science Bureau, Houston, Tex. 314
Social studies 216
Social work 314
Sociology 363, 396
South 26, 40, 50, 63, 65, 69, 91, 92, 93, 111, 126,
    130, 131, 132, 133, 134, 139, 165, 178, 205, 211,
    216, 218, 237, 244, 245, 280, 283, 299, 323, 332,
    334, 345, 361, 362, 366, 367, 368, 385, 386, 387,
    413, 421, 429, 432, 446
South Africa 7, 48, 59, 237, 304, 400, 401, 402
South America 180
South Carolina 223
  Aiken 256
  Charleston 355
  Columbia 272, 375
  St. Helena's Island 69, 70, 82, 87, 89
South Dakota Educational Association 365
South Philadelphia, Pa., High School for Girls 417
Southern Conference for Education and Industry 385
Southern Education Association 98, 366, 367, 368
Southern renaissance 216
Southern Rhodesia 369
Southern Tuberculosis Conference 249
Spelling 233
Spelman Seminary, Atlanta, Ga. 156
Standard Achievement scores 119
Standardization 196
Standards 330
Stanton-Arthur School, Philadelphia, Pa. 27
State 366
State agents for Negro schools 123, 146
State colleges 123, 128
State Department 410
Steamfitting 163
Strategic college centers 124
Strong, Alice C. 272
Students' Army Training Corps 170
Sudan 377, 378
Summer school 6, 298, 445
Superintendents, white 67

Supervision   67, 91, 92, 182, 195, 250, 298, 334, 383,
      411, 432
Survey of colleges and universities   384
Syrian Protestant College   185

Tailoring   163
Tanganyika   390, 391
Taxation   64, 74
Teacher training   6, 15, 47, 97, 110, 131, 135, 146,
      182, 240, 242, 245, 294, 299, 335, 350, 411, 432,
      444
Teachers   35, 183, 191, 326, 445, 456
Teachers College, Columbia University   237, 242, 302
Teachers' homes   108
Teaching load   245
Teaching methods   411, 431
Teaching profession   140, 205
Tennessee   39, 149
   Rutherford Co.   276
Term lengths   43, 432
Tests and measurements   86, 119, 127, 136, 137, 144,
      151, 205, 208, 209, 217, 222, 268, 272, 304, 317,
      344, 349, 374, 375, 379, 381, 382. *See also* names
      of specific tests
Texas, Houston   314
Textbooks   51, 246
Thorn, Charlotte   447
Tobago   405
Tolerance   113
Tonga   398
Trade schools   123
Trades   238, 393
Transportation   43, 108
Transvaal   400
Trinidad and Tobago   405
Tucker, A.E.   289
Tunisia   55
Tuskegee conferences   88
"The Tuskegee Idea"   31, 33
Tuskegee Institute   70, 78, 88, 215, 250, 251, 265,
      310, 321, 393, 437, 438

Uchee Valley School, Russell Co., Ala. 333
Uganda 407
United Free Church of Scotland 436
U.S. Bureau of Education 1, 2, 12, 22, 126, 169, 179, 384, 408, 409
U.S. Commission on Education in Haiti 400
U.S. Department of Agriculture 252
U.S. Department of State 410
U.S. Federal Bureau for Vocational Education 411
U.S. Office of Education 46, 47
Universal Races Congress 409
Universities in London 84
University Commission on Southern Race Questions 413, 414
University of Fez, Morocco 157
University of Georgia 184, 309
University of Habana, Cuba 341
University of Kansas 349
University of Pennsylvania 27
University of Texas 387
University of Virginia 363
Unskilled work 238
Urban League. See National Urban League
Urban students 435

Valena C. Jones Elementary School 440
Varona, E.J. 181
Verbal tests 382
Vermont State Teachers' Association 415
Vernacular 434
Village schools 110
Vineland Adjustment Score 304
Virginia 2, 5, 6, 18, 39, 141, 224, 248, 435, 439, 456
  Camp Lee 136
  Hanover Co. 83, 90, 118
  Lynchburg 383
  Norfolk 57
  Suffolk 36
  Tidewater 199
Virginia Conference of Charities and Correction 118

Virginia Education Commission 416
Virginia Industrial School 18
Virginia Industrial School for Colored Girls 83, 90
Virginia Manual Labor School for Colored Boys 83
Vocational buildings 108
Vocational education 32, 152, 325, 335, 410, 411
Vocational guidance 39, 247, 253, 259, 395
Vocations 54, 238, 435

Washington, Booker T. 25, 41, 79, 251, 274, 279,
    348, 385, 415
Washington monument, Tuskegee, Ala. 41
Weight 276
Welfare work 140
West Africa 7, 177, 434
West Virginia 35, 432, 449
West Virginia Collegiate Institute 35, 449
Wheelwrighting 163
White House Conference on Negro Schools 299
White people 43, 60, 67, 76, 137, 144, 173, 182,
    194, 205, 208, 217, 223, 226, 245, 265, 272, 276,
    295, 303, 309, 316, 320, 342, 359, 374, 375, 381,
    382, 433
William Penn School, South Carolina 69, 70, 82, 87,
    89
Women 331
Women teachers 35
Women's City Club of New York 210
Wood, Leonard 181
World Conference on Narcotic Education 262
World War I 28, 103
Wright, Arthur D. 85

Y.M.C.A. 248, 424
Yankee schoolma'ams 446
Yerkes test 381
Youth 341

Zanzibar 461

About the Author

Richard Newman is the compiler of several recent Black Studies reference books: *Lemuel Haynes: a bio-bibliography* (New York, Lambeth Press, 1984); *Black Access: a bibliography of Afro-American bibliographies* (Westport, Greenwood Press, 1984); *Black Index: Afro-Americana in selected periodicals, 1907-1949* (New York, Garland Publishing, 1982). With David W. Wills he co-edited *Black Apostles: Afro-Americans and the Christian mission from the Revolution to Reconstruction* (Boston, G.K. Hall, 1982).

Robert Morris, who wrote the introduction, is Head of Rare Books, Manuscripts, and Archives, the Schomburg Center for Research in Black Culture, The New York Public Library. He is the author of *Reading, 'riting and Reconstruction: the education of freedmen in the South, 1861-1870* (Chicago, University of Chicago Press, 1981).